Contents

Foreword

This collection both celebrates and challenges the nature of radicalism in adult education. As we enter the 1990s, the defining features of what is to count as 'radical' become more difficult to specify. In part this is because during the 1980s 'radical' was aligned with the Right, who through Thatcherism and beyond presented a new agenda for Britain, one tied to the market, managerialism and the concept of the active (consuming) citizen. Adult education, on the other hand, has had a clear and consistent debate with forms of left radicalism throughout its history and has generated an adult education tied to both the reformist and the more radical sections of the trade union movement.

Thus in 1991 we pause to consider where we have been and where we might be going. This consideration is, in fact, made more urgent by the recent publication of two White Papers detailing the future of further education and suggesting the end of the binary divide in higher education. Adult education has been simultaneously included in and excluded from the discussion. In relation to further education, the White Paper is an encouragement to overcome the vocational–non-vocational division in British education, yet there is no celebration of the way in which adult education has pre-empted this in what is called 'liberal adult education'. Instead, the White Paper appears to withdraw government support for adult education at the local authority level, while ignoring the contribution it makes to the university sector.

We find ourselves yet again facing another challenge to the ways in which adult education is inserted into the educational agenda and the ways in which it will be resourced. This is a good moment, therefore, to revive some of the earlier debates in the field. Much of this debate has centred around the critique of liberal adult education, individualism and the role of the market. The 1980s reinforced these themes but also presented new challenges in relation to the role of state intervention and the processes of restructuring, while the new social movements foregrounded a politics beyond the workplace and production relations in the contested arenas of feminism, movements for racial justice, peace, ecology and gay rights.

The papers brought together in this volume are both past and present, being in part articles from the journal *Studies in the Education of Adults* from the 1970s and 1980s, and contributions on the debates within adult education for those decades and into the 1990s by Teddy Thomas, Alan Tuckett and Sallie Westwood. Teddy Thomas and Sallie Westwood have both enjoyed the privilege of editing *Studies in the Education of Adults* during the 1980s and 1990s, contributing through this to the debates in the field. We hope with this collection to carry these debates further because they have a deep resonance with our current times, providing both memories and visions. We hope that the papers will be a stimulus to re-visioning radical agendas in the field.

Finally, our thanks to all the contributors for their co-operation in the production of this volume; to Christopher Feeney for his never-failing support; and to Ali Rattansi, with whom S.W. constantly discusses 'Radical Agendas?'.

S.W.
J.E.T.

Note: The articles from *Studies in the Education of Adults* are reproduced verbatim from the originals. The language used is highly gendered and privileges the masculine form. It seemed disingenuous to alter this.

Part I

Radical Agendas? Past, Present and Future

1

Innocence and After: Radicalism in the 1970s

J.E. THOMAS

This book sets out to examine the changes in British adult education between 1970 and 1990. It is concerned with the place of radicalism in those years, how it was perceived and what forms it took. The most recent contributions, in particular those of Sallie Westwood, pose the question: where is radicalism in the early 1990s? My own perspective is from university adult education, but there are no firm sectoral divisions in the papers collected here; indeed many celebrate the creative collaboration that was a feature of these years.

Developing a Stable Base

The two decades in question were serious ones for adult education, both for the hope and imagination with which adult educators pursued their goals, and for the potentially lethal consequences of the election of the Thatcher government in 1979. The threat to education was, of course, more general in its effects than is described here, but the eviction of Thatcher promises little consolation.

It is difficult to imagine, or even to recollect if one were in adult education at the time, its stability and promise in 1970. Many of the university departments were sizeable and well established. Some of the biggest were Leeds, Liverpool, Manchester and Nottingham (the latter was the oldest). Nothing illustrates the tumult of recent years more than the fact that three of these are a fraction of their former size, and in Liverpool its once large staff was moved to internal departments in 1990. But in 1970, adult educators discussed growth and new areas which might be developed and to which staff might be appointed. In this they were like other university departments, since, it will be remembered, the 1960s had witnessed an expression of value in the university system with the opening of several new universities, after the bold vision of the 1963 Robbins Report.

When it came to the question of what university adult educators actually did, it is doubtless the case that they continued to pursue what has often been called 'The Great Tradition'. In essence, this meant the provision of non-examinable courses of a high standard for members of the public. The underlying philosophy is one which can be traced to Plato, with his advocacy of an education which prepares for citizenship and teaches how to rule and to be ruled. In Britain the great advocates were Matthew Arnold, with his talk of culture as 'a pursuit of total perfection by means of getting to know ... the best which has been thought and said in the world'[1] and John Newman in *The Idea of a University*. It is from this that the central tradition in university adult education, most notably the rejection of a narrow, instrumental focus, derives:[2]

> *Some great men insist that education should be confined to some particular and narrow end and should issue in some definite work, which can be weighed and measured. They argue as if everything, as well as every person, had its price; and that where there has been a great outlay, they have a right to expect a return in kind. This they call making education and instruction 'useful' and 'utility' becomes their watchword. With a fundamental principle of this nature, they very naturally go on to ask, what there is to show for the expense of a university; what is the real worth in the market of the article called Liberal Education?*

The optimism of the late 1960s and early 1970s found expression too in the development of a theoretical base, and there were three notable examples of this. The first was the initiation and growth of academic courses in adult education. Practitioners who wished to reflect on their experience, to hear that of others, and to have the time and opportunity to get access to appropriate literature were now able to do so, and this remains an important part of university provision.

Concomitant with this opportunity for study and reflection, which rested upon the stability which was the hallmark of the period, was the growth of scholarly writing about adult education. At the end of the 1960s this growth encouraged the establishment of the first scholarly journal in Britain, *Studies in Adult Education*, and its successor *Studies in the Education of Adults*. Later in the decade there was established from a British base *The International Journal of Lifelong Education*. Finally, a small group of heads of university departments developed an organisational focus for this intellectual activity in the form of the Standing Committee on University Teaching and Research in the Education of Adults (SCUTREA), which came into being in 1970, and from that date has maintained a scholarly context which has attracted an international renown.[3]

The Radical Cause

Because university adult education was relatively well provided for, and because it generated intellectual activity, one of the questions which immediately dominated discussion was the purpose of it all. After all, it was agreed, if adult education was important, then it must seek some end. Did it seek to change people, or society, and if so, how? Should it ensure stability, or set as its goal the creation of instability? It was around this issue that debates about radicalism centred, and it is this issue which is addressed in the article by Harries-Jenkins and Thomas ('Adult education and social change', pages 109–120).

The debate was not new. The first and perhaps greatest controversy in Britain occurred very soon after adults were judged worthy of education. In 1908 a breakaway movement called the Plebs League was formed. The dissidents were students from the newly-founded Ruskin College in Oxford.[4] The cause of their dissatisfaction has been echoed many times since. It was that the education which they received was designed to bolster the status quo, was dishonest and took no account of the experience of 'ordinary' people. There was, one critic said: 'Nothing like education to draw away peoples' interest and sympathy from the wrongs and sorrows of the actual into an atmosphere of foggy and abstract idealism!'[5]

History has always been a particular target. The Horrabins, who were especially adamant critics of received versions of history, dismissed 'ruling class' ideas of education as propounded by the Greeks as irrelevant to the needs of workers.[6] Virginia Woolf, writing of women in history, pointed out: 'One is held up by scarcity of facts. One knows nothing detailed, nothing perfectly true and substantial about her. History scarcely mentions her'.[7] And in all countries, indigenous and minority groups have insisted upon history taking account of their place in it.

The radical 'cause' is not, therefore, new in debates about adult education. What is difficult to be certain of or to demonstrate is its extent both in intent and in practice. It was in an attempt to develop a model which would enhance the sophistication of debate that the article by Harries-Jenkins and Thomas appeared. The proposition is that the radical insists upon change at the roots of systems. Radicals do not want to 'improve' on the school system; they want to question whether or not it should exist. Similarly, education which improves the skills of trade unionists is not radical since the latter demands the right to question the desirability of trades unions. Nor, contrary to the abuse with which such claims are often met, are such demands doctrinaire. The constant theme in the history of claims for radicalism is that these claims are for truth. If history addressed itself to *truth*, then the unsatisfactory nature of society would be exposed. Reimer illustrates the ineffectiveness of usual educational assumptions and practice when he writes:

> *An educated minority of any size would never put up with current health and education services, environmental pollution, political policy control by military-industrial cliques or advertiser control of mass media, to say nothing of traffic jams, housing shortages and the host of other absurdities which afflict modern societies.*[8]

In the sense discussed above, radicalism is, in Weberian terms, an ideal type. This is why a continuum model of *tendencies* is proposed in the Harries-Jenkins/Thomas paper. The next rather less radical, but socially committed point along it is that of the reform position. Like the radical, the reformer measures success by manifest improvement in the quality of life in a society. The central difference between the two is that the reformer accepts that society is basically sound, but that it can be improved. The division or graduation between the two positions is extremely problematic, since intentions, proclamations, actions and subsequent claims for success have all to be taken into account.

The Community Development Movement

And so it is with some of the accounts of adult education in practice which are set out in this volume. One of these attracted a good deal of interest in the late 1960s and early 1970s, and this was community development. The notion of using education as a means of transforming the lives of communities, like so much in the British tradition, was not new, or notably British. Canon S.A. Barnett set up settlements in Victorian London specifically for this purpose, and Danilo Dolci has become a legend for his work among the dispossessed in Sicily. Indeed the classic example, and a formidable model, is the Antigonish movement in Canada, where M.M. Coady and J.J. Tomkins transformed the lives of poor fisherpeople through the establishment of co-operatives.[9]

Of special interest in the early 1970s were the attempts made to tackle the problems of what were categorised in the Plowden Report as Educational Priority Areas (EPAs). One of the best known of these efforts focused upon a poor area of Liverpool, and it is that effort which is the subject of the article by Lovett ('Adult and community education', pages 59–69). The key to such work is set out in his first paragraph, calling as it does for adult education to be seen 'as an integral part of a whole series of activities' based in the community. Lovett goes on to describe some of the kinds of activities in which he engaged:

the setting up of a claimants' union; establishment of a community centre; and organising a summer play group with parental involvement. Of great significance, as we shall see when outlining the alternative representative view by Paterson, is Lovett's assertion that: 'Formal courses . . . are impracticable and self-defeating.'

Whether or not this experiment, and others like it, can be fitted into the radical/reform continuum, there is no doubt that at the time it was a significant development for two reasons. Firstly, it was spearheaded by a *university* adult education department, and secondly because it appeared to be a notable, and rare, example of collaboration between such a department, the Local Education Authority, and the Workers' Educational Association. None of this meant that it was necessarily approved of, and evidence that it was not may be found in the almost total absence of any attempt to emulate its practice in other university departments or in the WEA.

This may have been because there had been, and at that time still was, a strong tradition which probably absorbed the energies of staff who might have been attracted to it. This was the formal work with trade unionists and with manual workers generally which was a feature of many departments.

Working-class Adult Education

There were and are adult educators who believe that their work should be directed at the historic working class, and who deplore, as Ward does in his article, the 'persistent middle-class bias of current adult education provision' ('A university adult education project with the unemployed', pages 123–135). Indeed, Fieldhouse demonstrates more than adequately the antiquity of that belief, and how it was a substantial source of the apprehension of the powerful ('Conformity and contradiction in English Responsible Body adult education, 1925–1950', pages 136–152). It is a common assumption that from the beginning, adult education was in some way concerned with the 'emancipation' of workers.

The structured programmes which could be found in many departments in the 1970s had a rather narrower focus than the 'emancipation' of whole classes and groups. A major area of work was the 'day release' scheme. Under such schemes, companies and nationalised industries allowed people to attend classes which ranged from general education to those specially designed for trade union officials. These had been a feature of provision for many years, and were especially singled out in the 1962 Annual Report of the Universities Council for Adult Education: 'It is the growing momentum throughout Great Britain of the day release courses for trade unionists that is one of the salient features of more recent years.'[10] The 'industrial tutors', as they were called, often organised substantial programmes, for example with the then National Coal Board, and there was a belief that the only successful way in which an impact could be made on industrial workers was through organisations, notably trade unions. It is certainly the case that the chances of gaining access to manual groups was very much greater with the support and encouragement of unions, backed by the authority of the employers. It is also, however, the case that such commitment as there was in the university departments to this kind of work was absorbed by these structured programmes, and deflected away from the much more difficult, and uncertain, engagement in community development.

The Critical Challenge

No account of the period would be accurate if the impression were created that this was a time of great radical activity. It was not. There were other views on how the resources of adult educational organisations should be deployed, and, by implication, the ideology which underlay that deployment.

The article by Paterson ('The concept of deprivation', pages 92–108) represents a substantial body of opinion in adult education which challenges the desirability and validity of engagement with social issues as a primary aim. In terms of volume, there were not many articles or books published during the two decades which would support Paterson's position, but that is no indication of how many university adult educators would agree with him. It is probable that those engaged in work with some kind of social purpose would be more likely to publish because of the unusual nature of what they were doing, and because they would seek to convert other people. There can be no doubt that Paterson's view is the one which lies behind most adult education in practice. Paterson acknowledges that the 'cluster of concepts' which includes deprivation 'in recent years have played an increasingly large part in discussions of educational aims and policy'. But he deplores the imprecision of such terms, and their use as 'emotive weapons'. In a closely argued article he suggests that the easy use of words like deprivation has led to a good deal of muddle-headed thinking, such as leaving out of account the fact that some people may be wilfully deprived of education through a conscious decision, what he terms 'the abstainers'. Indeed it is difficult to deny that this might explain the lack of interest in education in large parts of the population. On the other hand, the abstainers may be resisters who object to, and feel alienated from, an institutional framework which does not set out to cope with their needs.

Two articles published in *Studies in Adult Education* only a year before

Paterson's consider related issues, though with differing conclusions. See Harold C. Wiltshire, 'The concepts of learning and need in adult education'; and Kenneth H. Lawson, 'The justification of objectives in adult education', *Studies in Adult Education* 5, 1, 1973.

The Politicising of Adult Education

The transition from a stable situation, in which university adult educators were able to consolidate their experience, turn it to mutual advantage with their colleagues in other sectors and explore new and sometimes radical areas of work, was gradual. During the 1970s there were the first tentative efforts to organise courses for women, some of which adopted a common title, 'New Opportunities for Women'. By the late 1980s, the position of women in society, and the role of adult education in addressing itself to that position had become more urgent, as the article by Highet illustrates ('Gender and education', pages 153–166).

But the great trauma to the stability and promise of adult education in the 1970s came with the election of the Thatcher government of 1979. The disturbance to the equilibrium of British society was profound, but the attacks on the education system, and on adult education, although demoralising and destructive, paradoxically demonstrated how important education is. The fact that such a statement has to be made at all is a measure of the enormity of the attacks, but it is these attacks which have made education one of the most important political issues of the 1990s.

Among the first consequences of the Thatcher victory were considerable Conservative successes in local government in the next few years. When local authorities announced their much-vaunted cuts, a major target was the provision of adult education. This proved to be a serious mistake for it led to the establishment of a Save Adult Education Group, with support from all parts of both Houses of Parliament, and petitions to local authorities. The Nottinghamshire local education authority, for example, received some 6000 letters of protest, and the Conservative party lost control at the next election.

Local government did not affect the central government. In the latter, people believed that every malaise, from union 'agitation' to student misbehaviour, could be attributed to the inadequacy or the deliberately malignant ethos of the educational system. The authors of the Black Papers on education, published as a result of student unrest in 1968, could now feel their hour had come. Many of the contributions to those papers were regarded as variously pitiable or hilarious at the time,[11] but now it became clear that here was a government which was going to crush dissent. What was not properly appreciated was that its definition of dissent went a good deal farther than the subjugation of the left-wingers or anarchists (as the Black Papers would regard them). It meant the destruction of unions, erosion of civil liberties and, in the case of education, a series of sustained, irrational and, worst of all, erratic attacks.

The effect of cuts on funding on universities is now well documented and indisputable. These are susceptible to public gaze. What is not so visible is the atmosphere which now can be experienced in many university departments of adult education. Apart from the fact that there may not be the resources to engage in any radical activity, it is more than likely that any attempt to do so would now meet considerable disapproval and penalty. Not that this is new. Fieldhouse, in his article, reminds us of earlier resistance to non-conformist views, which are familiar indeed. Because of that resistance, adult education found itself:'Ultimately conforming to a rationalist and reformist consensus which kept "more extreme influences" at bay.'

He goes on to report how: 'a tutor's comments on the Amritsar massacre of 1919 led to protests about attacks on the government's Indian policy, and a visit from HMI "to examine Bruce closely about his views".' Fieldhouse also points out that the Colonial Office prevented 'suspect' lecturers from taking up extra mural posts in Africa.The Thatcher government and, as far as can be judged, its successor has, notoriously, engaged in centralising education. In respect of the education of adults this has taken the form of setting up a plethora of 'training agencies' which, since the early 1980s have been funded with money removed from other established educational agencies, and have been occupied in a series of Phoenix-like transformations of name, presumably in an attempt to establish credibility. Not only have they failed to do so, but there are other, more serious matters of concern. For these agencies, in addition to their political aim of concealing unemployment and their very questionable effectiveness, have been attended by administrative incompetence, and wholesale theft of public money.[12]

Whilst it is true that since 1979 education has operated in an especially quixotic and disagreeable environment, and there was destruction and wastage of ideas and talent which it will take years to appreciate, adult educators have now to consider what is to be done. They have to contemplate the last two decades, celebrate the achievements, reflect on the errors and identify the challenges.

Thus, when the government in the 1980s set out to destroy trade unionism, one of the great casualties was the National Union of Mineworkers. The smashing of this union in the Midlands led to the collapse of the trade unions work in several university departments and the WEA in respect of the day release classes described earlier. This kind of policy was one factor in the diminution, and in some areas the elimination, of that area of work which had been so significant in the past. Another was the incessant argument, much of it ideological, amongst staff and between staff and key organisations such as the TUC, which has descended, according to McIlroy, writing in 1988, into 'occasional bouts of open warfare.' He goes on to demonstrate how much energy was expended in this way: 'The consequences of struggles over what have been perceived by both sides as important and fundamental differences of philosophy and interest, rather than largely questions of resource allocation, have been unhappy ones.'[13]

The argument centred around a familiar theme, which is whether adult education should be liberal or functional. Staff in universities and the WEA believed in the former, and the TUC educators (or at least so it was alleged) believed in the latter. The first wanted to produce 'independent, critical, thinking trade unionists'[14] the latter 'company men', if trade unionists may be so described. TUC staff made, for the TUC, some odd, but familiar allegations, one of which was that a WEA tutor 'was preaching international socialist propaganda.'[15]

Perhaps the lesson to be learned from this is that people working in adult education should identify their unity of purpose, rather than too easily or too persistently split into factions. To do so is to expose oneself to ridicule, but a much greater danger lies in the ability of those in power to control, and if necessary, despatch those who seem to be incoherent. During the 1980s the potential for new animosities arose. There could be detected, without difficulty, demands for exclusivity in courses. Demands, for example, for courses only for women, or only for blacks. These demands have a long history, since in the 1970s there were many tutors who would, for example, teach only working-class students. This is a difficult issue, but the lessons of the 1980s ought to show that if there are good reasons for exclusivity in adult education (which claims to be universally desirable) then those reasons should be intelligible, and demonstrably so.

The Culture of Difference

There are other issues which require a good deal of consideration in the 1990s. One of these, addressed by Westwood in this volume, is racism, and more generally, cultural diversity ('Constructing the other' pages 167–173). There is perhaps no better example of the change in the challenge of adult education than the fact that in the 1970s, and for much of the 1980s, the issue of racism was very rarely discussed in adult education journals. This is perhaps an especially difficult challenge because it is still outside the intellectual and practical experience of many who work in adult education. Her article demonstrates the persisting nature of ethnic identity and division, and the hideous ethnic violence of Europe in recent years chillingly illustrates the point. Perhaps the classic radical struggle against capitalism will be rivalled by an equally radical attempt through adult education to encourage the view that cultural diversity is the great new reality of our age and that we have to learn to live with people through difference.

Such admonitions should not imply that adult educators are inflexible. On the contrary, they have always demonstrated flexibility and susceptibility to new ideas. The article by Ward illustrates this. In it he discussed work with the unemployed, and his claims are as resolute as such claims were in the 1970s: 'Secondly, it has to be recognised that most of the unemployed are working-class people living in relative poverty, and that education must help them in this situation'.

Starting from a premise 'that unemployment is now structural', he goes on to describe a project to tackle it. The aims are twofold. Firstly, to open access to the unemployed to the liberal studies programme which has always been the backbone of adult education, and, secondly, to help the unemployed to understand the nature of their situation and how it may be ameliorated. Nor has the faith in engaging the more dispossessed parts of the community in education disappeared, as the article by Head shows ('Education at the bottom', pages 70–91). This is an account of an attempt to engage in educational activities with the most 'difficult' groups, members of which, as Head fairly observes, would not be welcomed in the more usual class.

Even in the short time between the work of Lovett and Head, one can detect changes in the mood of adult education. Head is perhaps rather more realistic than earlier writers. He observes that education is a 'bonus activity for the deprived', but he wrote at a time when the views of Ivan Illich seemed convincing. Illich[16] had told us how awful educational institutions were, how they created divisions and misery rather than, as had been supposed, leading to happiness and fulfilment. At the peak of Illich's popularity it was possible to conjure up nightmares of relentless harassment by adult educators. For adult educators who believed in the transforming nature of adult education, Illich's work presented a critical dilemma.

In Head's article there is much talk of cultural 'invasion', again reflecting the increasing importance to adult educators of the work of Paolo Freire, at the end of the 80s without doubt the most important influence on adult educators, or at least the most precocious.[17] The central contribution made by Freire is to admonish against assault on the values of groups which are different from those of the adult educator. Freire's other admonition is to start the learning process from the position of the learner, with all the profound implications which follow from that. So Head, as did many adult educators in the 1980s, recognises that he is dealing with another culture, in his case 'the subcultures of impotence', and that the work of Illich and Freire restrains confidence in handling a newly recognised problem.

The total effect of this is that Head is altogether less dogmatic than earlier practitioners about what should be done, and this uncertainty became a common theme in discussion at the end of the 1980s. Nevertheless, Head is not pessimistic, for like Lovett he sees room for action, even as modest as preparing a letter complaining about the quality of a hostel.

Head's article is, in several respects, a good focus for assessing the last two decades. He expresses a concern for the quality of life in society, modifies his optimism with reflection on experience, and draws upon the intellectual development which has become a crucial aspect of adult education in recent years.

There is indeed reason for adult educators to be optimistic in the 1990s. Although some of the biggest university departments may have gone or been reduced in size, several new departments have been established. The intellectual base is flourishing and academic courses continue to develop. Continuing education, in the sense of professional updating provides more and new opportunities, and mature students are at the centre of the Access plans developed by many institutes of higher education. All of which demonstrates that adult education has survived the worse assaults in its history, and is winning.

References

1. M. Arnold, *Culture and Anarchy*, Cambridge: Cambridge University Press, 1932, p 6.
2. J.H. Newman, *The Idea of a University*, Longmans, Green & Co., 1901, pp 92–93.
3. For an account of SCUTREA see J.E. Thomas, 'Adult education research and SCUTREA', *Studies in the Education of Adults* 16, 1984.
4. For an account of this famous upheaval see B. Jennings, 'Revolting students: the Ruskin College dispute 1908–9', *Studies in Adult Education* 9, 1, 1977.
5. 'Ivan the Fool', *Fellowship* IV, 8, 1918, ed. F. Sinclaire. Reprinted in A. Wesson (ed.), *Basic Readings in Australian Adult Education*, Melbourne: Council of Adult Education, 1971.
6. J.F. and W. Horrabin, *Working Class Education*, Labour Publishing Co., 1924, p 71.
7. V. Woolf, *A Room of One's Own*, Hogarth Press, 1949, p 67.
8. E. Reimer, *School is Dead*, Penguin Books, 1971, p 138.
9. For an account of their work see their entries in J.E. Thomas and B. Elsey (eds), *International Biography of Adult Education*, Nottingham: University of Nottingham Department of Adult Education, 1985.
10. For a detailed account of this work see John McIlroy, 'Storm and stress: the Trades Union Congress and university adult education 1964–1974', *Studies in the Education of Adults* 20, 1, 1988.

11. For an especially philistine and representative article see K. Amis, 'Pernicious participation', in C.B. Cox and A.E. Dyson (eds), *Fight for Education: a Black Paper*, The Critical Quarterly Society, 1969.

12. A typical account of fraudulent behaviour is given in *The Independent* 2 February 1991, p 6.

13. McIlroy, op.cit. p 61.

14. ibid., p 66.

15. ibid., p 67.

16. I. Illich, *Deschooling Society*, Calder and Boyers, 1971.

17. P. Freire, *Pedagogy of the Oppressed*, Penguin Books, 1972.

2

Counting the Cost: Managerialism, the market and the education of adults in the 1980s and beyond

ALAN TUCKETT

The disciplines of the market came early to adult education, but it has taken a decade of government commitment to narrowly instrumental priorities in educational policy for adult educators to adapt their language to take account of externally imposed changes. The pressures to reduce public expenditure have continued relentlessly since the early 1970s. As Margaret Thatcher argued in July 1978: 'If our objective is to have a prosperous and expanding economy, we must recognise that high public spending, as a proportion of GNP, very quickly kills growth . . . Every penny they take is taken from the productive sector of the economy in order to transfer it to the unproductive part of it.'[1] It is not surprising, therefore, that local government was a key target in the struggle to reduce public spending, and although there is little to suggest that the analysis is right, it dominated public policy for much of the 1980s.[2]

Paying for Learning

As a largely discretionary area of expenditure, local education authority adult education, which remains the largest sector of provision for adult learners, has suffered disproportionately from reductions in local authority finance. Already by 1978 Wiltshire and Mee were expressing serious concern about the pressure to make student fees cover tuition costs: 'The danger is that when a position like this is established it becomes very difficult to retreat from it: what begins as an emergency measure becomes a principle which nobody questions.' They noted that: 'Over considerable parts of the country adult education is now regarded not as part of the public education system but as an optional extra which those who want must pay for, and which is available only to those who can pay; the role of the educational service becomes that of the provider of accommodation and some administrative support for self-financing leisure activities.' They concluded that these changes add up to a radical shift of policy, which was, in 1978, little remarked: 'Among adult educators the general feeling seems, quite understandably, to be one of helplessness.'[3]

In his introductory essay for the 1980–81 *Year Book* of the National Institute of Adult Education, Arthur Stock traced a loss of status in education during the 1970s back to the 'gross overclaims of the 1960s', and to the introduction of corporate management in local government, and commented that: 'A completely unfair spin-off of this unfortunate attitude shift was the transfer in categorisation of adult education from an investment good into a consumer good, and the equating of most out-of-school education with leisure activity.'[4]

Reviewing pressures likely to face local authority services in the 1980s, Stock remarked: 'There is a growing demand from many elected members that what they call (quite inaccurately) the "non-statutory" part of education should go to the market place, sell its wares as any other leisure/recreational industry and find its resources from the margins achieved from the consequent trading activity. There is a partial (though by no means total) acceptance by these politicians that there may be certain types of social-priority adult education which would warrant an allocation of public finance. But, so this caucus would state, all or most of the other costs such as organising the programmes, teaching the students, providing the materials, paying for the accommodation, servicing the capital, should be met by fees or possibly by sponsorships and special fund raising.'[5]

The change in policy clearly perplexed adult educators. Mee and Wiltshire observed that the traditional low-fee economy in adult education 'was an element in our educational system of which we could be proud and which colleagues in other countries admired and envied.'[6] Stock deprecated the 'unfortunate' attitudes of corporate management, the 'quite inaccurate' assumptions among politicians about the legal status of adult education, and the ways in which 'this caucus' of politicians sought to introduce the disciplines of the market to adult education. Instead, he felt, the onus should be on the politicians to understand the complexity of the system, and the value of adult education in Britain, as our colleagues abroad do.[7]

Engaging with Local Politics

In 1979, staff from two Responsible Bodies in the East Midlands set out to put the politicians right. The Save Adult Education Campaign was initially established to contest two decisions made by Nottinghamshire Education Committee, to increase fees sharply, to just under double the national average, with no exemptions for any category of students, and to take all but 30 schools out of evening use. Eighty-six per cent of the classes planned in the county were cut as a result of these decisions and Responsible Body provision was severely disrupted. In part, Nottinghamshire's decision was in response to the newly-elected Conservative government's call for cutbacks in council expenditure. However, the local campaign was concerned, too, that some of the impetus resulted from the restructuring of provision for adult learners. As Kenneth Lawson explained: 'There is a strong suspicion locally that these moves . . . are part of a longer term strategy which began three years ago when the organisation of adult education was based on the Colleges of Further Education. At that time, Area Principals were abolished and many misgivings were expressed.'[8]

Despite attracting 400 students to a public meeting, flooding the press and local media with reasoned criticism of the proposals and public demonstrations at the doors of County Hall, the campaign did not succeed in preventing the cuts in Nottinghamshire from going through, although the leader of the Conservative group on the council was quoted as saying that members were aware of the reaction the cuts had provoked and that although economies had to be made, the Council was prepared 'to think again.' Over the next decade, whilst Nottinghamshire completed the re-structuring of its adult education service into colleges, resources for adult learners have been comparatively well protected. Lawson drew one key lesson from the campaign: 'That protest against cuts in adult education crosses Party lines and a strict non-party platform is essential. A great asset in securing political neutrality is the existence of a free-standing organisation such as the East Midlands Regional Institute which has funds at its disposal, a number of activists and no particular axe to grind. The support of the staff of the Responsible Bodies who are not directly affected by the cuts is also invaluable.'[9] After a decade of confident, ideological government, in which partisanship was celebrated, as long as you were 'one of us', Lawson's conclusion seems to come from a by-gone era. And in the campaigns of the 1980s to defend the Inner London Education Authority, it was those students who were also partisan Conservative ward members in Wandsworth and Westminster, anxious to protect their adult education classes, who did much to prolong the life of the authority, and to sustain the rich diversity of its adult service.

The Save Adult Education Campaign became a national organisation in November 1979, held a meeting at the House of Commons with sympathetic MPs in December, leading to the creation of an all-party parliamentary group for adult education, and culminated in September 1980 in a rally in Trafalgar Square. The Advisory Council for Adult and Continuing Education added its voice to concerns about cutbacks in spending, and in November 1979, the journal *Adult Education* described local education authorities as running 'butcher shop administrations based on primitive arithmetic.' Nevertheless, cuts, and re-structuring of local education authority services for adult learners continued unabated.[10]

In East Sussex, in the lead-up to the 1981–2 budget, the council proposed to cut all expenditure (some £600,000) on adult education, on the grounds that 'people don't want to pay for tap-dancing on the rates.' I was working then at the Friends Centre, a small voluntary centre in Brighton, which received a tiny but vital core grant from the local education authority. Tired, like many other adult educators, of writing begging letters to businesses and charities, or chasing the latest version of short-life funding from the Manpower Services Commission, tired, too, of raising student petitions and producing arguments against cuts, we decided to try to raise money for our centre, and to demonstrate the cultural power embedded in groups of adults learning, by organising a non-stop Teach-In.

The teach-in ran from 9 o'clock on Monday morning, until 9 o'clock on Saturday evening during one week in February, 1981. We asked tutors to offer one free session, making their work accessible to students, asked students to pay anything they wanted for attending classes, and sought sponsorship at a penny an hour for the whole event as long as someone was studying throughout the period. Pensioners painted the night away, taking a first opportunity to paint urban night-life; astronomers used the garden throughout the week; I taught an all-night history of rock music attended by eighty-five people; thirty others turned up at 6 am for a celebration of Jean-Paul Sartre. There was a peace conference, a *Messiah* sing-in; the producer of the BBC drama serial *Sons and Lovers* explained the process of starting with a budget and ending with a television series; there were safe experiments with animals; laser beam technology; graffiti boards; a magazine made by the full-time basic education students taking a TOPS Preparatory course. People went to classes, swept the corridors, served in the canteen, and went home and saw themselves on television. Partly because the event combined some elements of the bizarre with elements of serious arguments about public expenditure, television and radio gave the event a great deal of coverage, enough to persuade a family from the Orkneys to drive down and spend their week's holiday at the event. By the end of the week, the Friends Centre had raised enough money for short-term survival, the council changed its policy, and the leader announced that he had been badly advised. More importantly, the culture of the Friends Centre was transformed, as students recognised their own agency, and the importance of learning together whatever they wanted to learn.[11]

Within two years, the local education authority was again chipping away at adult education budgets, bearing out Stock's view that government, central and local, could no longer be persuaded that spending on liberal, general, multi-purpose adult education was an investment good. If people wanted to spend leisure-time activity on learning of this sort, they would need to pay for it themselves. This sentiment was captured succinctly in Councillor Green's assertion that 'people don't want to pay for tap-dancing on the rates'. It is an interesting statement. It suggests that the people who matter don't go to adult education classes, or that if they do they would recognise the unfairness of adding to the rates burden of other local residents. It separates adult learning from serious education, which people would, with a greater or lesser degree of enthusiasm, agree to pay for on the rates. Who then, is adult education catering for? It is, the statement suggests, for people seeking frivolous diversion at the rate-payer's expense.

Who Participates?

In responding to that charge, adult educators were not entirely helped by the gap between the rhetoric and the practice of 'this great movement of ours.' The professionals always took pride in arguing that adult education offered the first serious opportunity for sustained study to many people who had been failed in their initial education, yet research consistently showed that the service was much better at attracting people who had enjoyed prolonged and successful initial education than it was in reaching school drop-outs, better at recruiting middle-class participants than working-class adults. After fifty years of celebrating the merits of study for its own sake, it was disquieting to confront evidence that black and working-class people wanted clear, instrumental outcomes from their studies, and that many found adult education centres unwelcoming places.

The pressure to make cuts or to charge students a higher proportion of the costs of their studies was resisted in some places. In the cities, and particularly in inner London, Sheffield and Manchester, funding for the education of adults was protected and increased. Some rural authorities, too, continued to expand the range and accessibility of provision. However, the early 1980s sharply increased the differences in provision between different parts of the country, and between different authorities in the same part of the country. Radical political leaderships in the cities encouraged adult educators to develop programmes for those people who had benefited least from previous education, and to target all provision to increase their participation. This policy thrust was reinforced by the central government money made available to inner city authorities for community initiatives in the light of the 1981 riots.

In high-spending authorities, the key question in programme planning and evaluation was 'Who participates?' The political priorities of authorities with policies in sharp contrast to those of central government combined with debates in adult education provision about the lessons of the 1973 Russell Report to encourage organisers and teachers to defend the liberal tradition in specific targeted provision for one or other of the groups enumerated in the Russell Report[12] and in Peter Clyne's *The Disadvantaged Adult*.[13] The adult literacy campaign of the 1970s was the first illustration of this. Literacy work emerged from voluntary contexts in which private, one-to-one teaching and learning was undertaken by students and volunteers, to be claimed as a central part of the curriculum of adult education centres and institutes. At its best this move was accompanied by the development of student-centred, discussion-based group work in which students and tutors negotiated what was to be written and read, reading the world as a precursor to reading words. Such work provoked periodic public enquiries into alleged political bias in the curriculum offered in particular centres. Decision makers were surprised by the energy and vitality of programmes of study centred in the lives and strong words of a group of learners who had previously felt that education was for other people.[14] Nevertheless, it has been instructive to see the shift during the 1980s away from uncertificated open study towards the accreditation of basic skills work and the development of workplace basic education.

Provision of English classes for people who were permanently settled in Britain followed literacy work as a key focus for curriculum development in urban adult education services. English as a Second Language courses were distinguished from courses for European tourists in their focus on a survival curriculum that included the language needed for claiming benefit, seeking asylum, information about housing rights and arrangements for education. They were as concerned with education about cultural difference as with language acquisition. During the 1980s ESL provision underwent rapid development and change, including a change of name (English for Speakers of Other Languages) and the development of certificated provision and language support strategies to ensure access to the full range of post-school education and training.

Outreach programmes sought to counteract the narrow subject-centred offer of many adult education programmes by negotiating learning with people on their own terms, in places of their own choice. However, the perspective of the outreach worker can have an important effect on shaping the outcome of negotiation. As Sally Nicholls and Evelyn Murray asked, in a paper reviewing community education developments in ILEA:

> *If we are genuinely assessing priority needs in different geographical areas of London, why do we all come up with such similar formulae, e.g., activities for mothers and toddlers? Yes, we consider this group as a priority group throughout the Inner City; but it is also an acceptable group that is relatively easily found and gathered together, fairly highly motivated and on the whole attractive and lively! Do we give less priority to groups who are less easily identified, contacted and organised, less highly motivated and less attractive, e.g., drop-outs?[15]*

Adult education provision has always been mainly women's education. Women account for almost three-quarters of adult education enrolments.[16] Low status, uncertificated work, often under-resourced, and attracting few grants, it has, nevertheless offered space for many women to reflect on their experience, and to reshape their lives. It is not surprising that much of the work developed with working-class communities, outside the boundaries of traditional centre-based programmes, has targeted and attracted women. Nor is it surprising that return to study courses for women have been a major growth element in centre-based programmes, as adult education centres have sought to contribute to the evolution of access routes to educational and training opportunities.

Equal Opportunities

Perhaps the most important change prompted by the combination of changed central government policies and the emerging commitment of local education authorities to equality of opportunity has been the development of strategies to open the whole of post-compulsory education to adult learners. During the 1980s adult education stopped being synonymous with night school, yet vocabulary inhibited widespread recognition of the changes that made adult learners a majority of the participants in further and higher education as a whole. The development of strategies to support student progression between different institutions and sectors of education depended on the active participation of staff working in different organisations on a number of related but distinct initiatives. Post-school education and training is extremely complex in the range of overlapping programmes offered and the bewildering variety of qualifications offered. The development of educational guidance and advice services has been an important component of improving progression opportunities, though such services are scantily resourced, whether as independent bodies or as aspects of institutional provision, for the scale of need.[17] A second key development has been the creation of accreditation-based Open

College networks, to enable workers in different institutions to recognise and accredit learning undertaken in a wide variety of contexts, and complementing the National Council for Vocational Qualifications, which seeks to create a coherent system of vocational qualifications.[18,19] Higher education institutions, facing the prospect of declining student numbers resulting from the 35% drop in the size of the 18-year-old population between the late 1980s and early 1990s, made links with local further education colleges to create full-time Access courses to attract mature students into higher education. Access courses grew rapidly to total more than 600 courses by the end of the 1980s, in almost all local authorities and across a wide range of subjects, with some degree of national coherence afforded by the CNAA Access Courses Recognition Group. These courses, the network of return to study programmes and the slow development of opportunities for adults to have their prior experience and learning assessed and accredited have extended the range of facilities available to adult learners in the 1980s in many local education authority areas, despite the pressure on finances.

In all of this, the principles of liberal adult education, of encouraging broad-based, critical enquiry that builds on the experience students bring to their learning with a plurality of learning and teaching strategies, have been central. Initiatives to change the pattern of provision for people with disabilities have drawn on the growing confidence of the organisations run by people with disabilities. Similarly, the development of women's studies in the last fifteen years and the more recent development of black studies have been more responsive to cultural changes outside educational institutions than to the priorities of local education authorities or of central government. Support for community action and community development, such as that fostered by the Greater London Council's Popular Planning Project, has shown that jobs based on needs can be created by imagination, planning and identifying resources, and that the skills of the venture capitalist can be learned, and transformed by local communities.[20]

In their attempts to secure equality of opportunity many students and potential students confront the arthritis of bureaucracy; the accumulation of barriers to access enshrined in rules and regulations, custom and practice. Much of the equal opportunities work in adult education in the 1980s sought to address these issues, and through the measures adopted, policy-makers, staff and students sought to transform the structures in which they work.

Restructuring Adult Education

1. LEA Provision

The effect of central government policy, when combined with local pressures to improve equality of opportunities, has been to re-structure much liberal education in many local education authorities into clearly targeted provision aimed at specific groups of people, and often requiring a substantial time commitment from students. However, these changes have not been universal. The gap between adult education services in urban, well-resourced, culturally plural Britain and the under-funded services on offer in much of rural Britain is striking, and grew for much of the decade, though the closure of the ILEA in 1989 has done much to weaken the most developed programmes.[21]

One universal impact on local education authority provision has been the ending of the unplanned, demand-led growth of traditional two-hours-a-week provision. There was for most of the 1980s some narrowing of curriculum offer, but a remarkable resilience in student recruitment, perhaps because the general adult education offer is a relatively inexpensive option in the leisure market for that majority of students in well-paid, secure work. The failure of that programme and its pricing mechanism to meet the needs of unemployed and under-employed adults without special funding is, however, easy to demonstrate in much of the country.

2. The Workers' Educational Association

The government's approach to the Workers' Educational Association was in the early part of this period strikingly different to its treatment of local education authorities. Rhodes Boyson, the junior minister responsible for adult education in the 1979 government, described the WEA as 'the greatest product of adult education',[22] and, perhaps under his benign influence, the DES compensated WEA districts for the loss of grants resulting from the local education authorities' financial crisis, with the effect that central government grants to the Association doubled in a period when inflation increased by only 50%. By 1983, however, the government's belief that users of services should bear a higher proportion of the costs of services led to a review of funding arrangements, and to what Brendan Evans describes as a 'three-fold cut.' Having recovered surpluses from the small number of WEA Districts which did not make a loss in 1983, the government proposed to reduce grant aid to the WEA by 8.3% in stages over three years, and expected the WEA to compensate for loss of grant by increasing student fees. This cut coincided with a reduction of almost 15% in funding for university extra-mural departments, who passed on a proportion of their cuts to the WEA, and continuing pressure on local authority finances led local education authorities to cut back on grant to the WEA.

However, the 1983 proposals did more than cut grants. They encouraged Districts to compete with each other for finite resources, and to give greater value to profit generation than to student recruitment.[23] Despite detailed negotiations and some modification to the original proposals, the 1984 financial arrangements produced difficulties for the WEA throughout the late 1980s, with some Districts experiencing recurrent deficits. However, they exposed the weakness of the Association's fiscal control through its decentralised and federal structure. These issues came to a head with the financial collapse of the Southern District of the Association. A further review of the Association and its finances was undertaken by the DES, and the WEA responded to the situation by agreeing, at its 1989 biennial conference, to a change in structure, to enable the Association to receive its funding from government centrally. No sooner was this agreed than the government announced a new initiative, designed to bring the work of the Association more closely into contact with local education authority provision by shifting funding from the Department to local education authorities, firstly through the mechanism of an Education Support Grant, and eventually through the rate support grant. If this proposal had been implemented unamended, its effect would have been to weaken seriously the central co-ordinating function of the Association, since local education authorities can hardly have been expected to vote tight finances for the maintenance of the national office. Once again, negotiation ameliorated the worst effects of the proposals by the time the changes were introduced in 1990.

However, the twists and turns of central government relations with the WEA make clear the lack of consistency and of clarity of government thinking about the role of the voluntary sector in the education of adults. While the inter-departmental review of government's relations with the voluntary sector was widely welcomed for its understanding of the complementary role of the voluntary sector, the DES seemed throughout the decade to alternate between a desire to manage and co-opt the voluntary sector and a wish to simplify its own structures, de-centralising messy and complex responsibilities to local government.[24]

3. Higher Education

Government policy in local education authority and WEA provision was driven by the belief that users of services should pay a higher proportion of their costs. In higher education, this policy can be seen in the pressure on extra-mural departments to reduce costs in 1984, and in the legislation to introduce student loans, but government policy in this area was driven by another imperative. From early in the decade, there was a recognition that demographic change was likely to have an impact on student numbers entering higher education from 1986 onwards. The recruitment of mature students into degree bearing courses and the resulting encouragement of Access courses were key priorities which did much to shape government thinking about adult learners in higher education. In 1984, Noel Thompson, Under-Secretary with responsibility for adult education in the DES, contrasted the timidity and insularity of British extra-mural provision with the success of American community colleges in attracting widespread adult participation across the full range of their activities.

The importance of adult learners in higher education was equally recognised by higher education institutions themselves. The NAB/UGC Standing Committee on Continuing Education referred to Continuing Education as a fifth Robbins Principle for Higher Education:

> *Continuing Education needs to be fostered not only for its essential role in promoting economic prosperity but also for its contribution to personal development and social progress. It can renew personal confidence, regenerate the human spirit and restore a sense of purpose to people's lives through the cultivation of new interests. In short, both effective economic performance and harmonious social relationships depend on our ability to deal successfully with the changes and uncertainties which are now ever present in our personal and working lives. That is the primary role which we set for continuing education.* [25]

The tone of the statement is confident, particularly in its defence of the function of education in fostering personal development, and in building personal confidence. In this, it is in stark contrast to much political debate about adult learning in the 1980s, which concentrated on the narrowly instrumental. However, the effects of funding changes on extra-mural work in universities has been to diminish opportunities for learning that explicitly seeks those goals. Liberal education without certification, designed to foster critical understanding, has been under fiscal pressure in higher education in the same way that it has been under pressure in local education authorities and the WEA. At the same time as continuing education as a sector has seen an overall increase in funding, with the transfer of its budget from the DES to the Universities Funding Council, liberal adult studies have declined, with major reductions and programme closures in Liverpool and Hull.

4. Access Courses

The most significant developments of the decade in higher education have been led by the polytechnics, particularly in the expansion of Access course provision. The initial impetus for Access courses came from the ILEA, and derived from its equal opportunities policy commitments, and its willingness to seek the implementation of those policies through its substantial funding of the five inner London polytechnics. Courses linking higher education institutions to colleges, and more unusually adult education institutes, sought to target student groups under-represented in the higher education student body. CNAA research showed that mature students, recruited through Access courses, out-performed 18-year-old entrants with conventional A-level entry qualifications.[26] However, further CNAA research undertaken by Wolverhampton Polytechnic demonstrated that unless Access courses were specifically targeted the social, gender and ethnic profile of students recruited through Access courses exactly paralleled those recruited through conventional routes.[27]

Many of the innovations introduced in public sector higher education were modified versions of initiatives pioneered by the Open University at the start of the 1970s. It is a striking feature of the political debate about higher education in Britain and of institutional discussion that the experience and achievements of the Open University are still so little recognised.

By the end of the decade it was clear that anxieties about the supply of 18-year-old entrants had been exaggerated. Whilst the overall age cohort shrank by 35% from the mid-1980s to the early 1990s, the number of children born to professional and managerial families, from whom higher education has traditionally recruited, grew by 10%. At the same time, participation rates increased sharply. The window of opportunity for adult learners was closing. That it had not altogether shut was a result of the third major policy imperative.

Towards a Learning Workforce

Every major commentator agrees that the British workforce is under-skilled, under-educated and under-trained, and that increasingly international markets, shorter job-life, and skill shortages in key economic sectors make adult training and education a major imperative. Throughout the 1980s the Manpower Services Commission (and its later manifestations, the Training Commission, the Training Agency and the Employment Department's Training, Enterprise and Education Directorate) and to a lesser extent the DES sought to influence the practice of educational providers to improve their relationships with and service to industry. The New Vocationalism of the 1980s was driven by a large number of government initiatives, each in its way seeking to improve the fit between the labour supply needs of industry and delivery in the education service. Geoffrey Melling and Geoff Stanton identified four key programmes which targeted adult workers, seeking to attract them to upgrade their skills: PICKUP; REPLAN; the Adult Training Strategy, the Job Training Scheme and Employment Training; and the Open Tech and later the Open College.[28] The role of the MSC in pushing local education authorities to engage in formal planning of work-related further education, and, later, to prepare schemes for all further education provision may also be seen to have had a major impact on adult learning opportunities.

1. PICKUP

PICKUP (Professional, Industrial and Commercial Updating) offers support to colleges, polytechnics and universities in meeting the updating and retraining needs of employers and their workers, usually at 'full cost'. It has helped to introduce the idea that customers of training and education are not always the same as students. It has introduced a far wider range of academic staff in post-compulsory education to adult learners. However, Her Majesty's Inspectors' report on PICKUP initiatives in 1988, while praising the technical content and customised design of institutions' PICKUP initiatives, suggested that institutions were weak on teaching and learning methodologies appropriate to adult learners.[29] In part, this may have been because of the initial reaction of many adult educators in regarding the PICKUP initiative as training rather than education. In much of the writing about issues affecting adult learners, the end of the vocational and non-vocational divide is celebrated, but it has a habit of lingering on, regardless.

2. REPLAN

REPLAN and the various Manpower Services Commission initiatives targeting adults shared in common a concern to address the learning needs of unemployed adults. The price of the sharp recession of 1979–81, and the restructuring of the British economy was large-scale and long-term unemployment, peaking at more than three million people registered unemployed, to which need to be added many others looking for work or under-employed. What distinguished the programmes was that REPLAN concentrated on those things that could most successfully encourage a readiness to learn, whilst the MSC initiatives were for most of the decade more narrowly instrumental. That the DES should establish two programmes, PICKUP and REPLAN, with a labour market focus, without involving the MSC in their plans, is evidence of the difficulty the Employment Department and the DES had in working together throughout the 1980s. The larger issue is the inability of the government to secure holistic social policy planning.

REPLAN was established in 1984, to give impetus to educational initiatives for the unemployed. The bulk of the programme was delivered through the National Institute of Adult Continuing Education, and through the project programme of the Further Education Unit. It was distinguished not so much by its early concentration on short-term project funding, but by its concern to help institutions, and in particular further education colleges, to address the barriers to participation experienced by unemployed adults. Watts and Knasel established early in the life of the programme five key benefits an education programme offers unemployed people: a time-structure to the day; regularly shared experiences and contacts with people outside the family; links to wider goals and structures; a new status and identity, that of 'learner'; a stimulus to activity.[30]

Over seven years, however, the REPLAN programme made clear that many of the provisions that work well for unemployed people are also pre-requisites for the successful recruitment, retention and progression of working-class people in general. Of course, REPLAN has also been able to point to activities with an immediate impact on the labour market, as in the stimulation of market gardening in Peterlee, but perhaps its key achievement has been in translating the concerns and needs of unemployed adult learners to institutional providers and to employers.[31]

3. MSC Programmes

There is a marked contrast between the priorities of the Manpower Services Commission at the beginning of the 1980s and its concerns at the beginning of the 1990s. At the beginning of the period there was large-scale youth unemployment and growing adult unemployment. By the end of the period there had been a dramatic increase in part-time employment, large numbers of women had entered the labour market, and Britain was facing a combination of skills and labour shortages. The MSC has consistently analysed the balance of needs of employers with the aspirations of workers in the policy discussion that has accompanied its major changes of programme affecting adults. In the consultative document *A New Training Initiative* issued in May 1981, the Commission identified four kinds of need that would not be met by improving arrangements for the supply of young workers:

1. Growing numbers of adults with relatively few skills or with skills restricted to a narrow range of manual operations or office tasks are needing a chance to make a fresh start through accelerated training for jobs in growth sectors.
2. Growing numbers of those with competences which have become outdated or rusty through lack of practice are seeking retraining or refresher courses.
3. Growing numbers of skilled people are looking for progression to more demanding or responsible work.
4. Firms and individuals alike are seeking means of responding rapidly to new demands. In such cases, adults need additional modules of skill and knowledge to graft on to existing competence.[32]

The 1983 discussion paper *Towards an Adult Training Strategy*[33] expanded this analysis and also gave some recognition to the case for special measures for people with particular needs (whether resulting from disability, language needs or basic skills), the importance of access to information and advice, and the importance of partnership between training and further and higher education bodies.

As an analysis of the tasks facing the British economy in creating a more skilled and flexible workforce, these statements stand up well. It is, however, hard to see how the policy changes adopted by the government arising from the New Training Initiative and from the Adult Training Strategy could be expected to meet the needs identified here. In part this resulted from the assumption that all adult training for employed people should be employer-led and self-financing, with government intervention limited to start-up grants and possible loan schemes. This clearly would not work for the growing numbers of unemployed people. The government's main response to the growth in adult unemployment was the introduction of the Community Enterprise Programme, expanded in October 1982 to the Community Programme, which was by April 1984 catering for 113,000 people, and at its peak in 1986 for 250,000. The programme provided temporary part-time or full-time work on projects of benefit to the community for long-term unemployed people. It aimed to improve 'employability by providing work experience, training (in some cases) and a recent work reference from an employer.'[34] However, the brackets are important. In practice the Community Programme was designed to provide inexpensive alternative sources of labour for marginal activities, and was not sufficiently well-funded to secure access to training for the mass of its participants.

4. Employment Training

The Community Programme was complemented in 1986 by the introduction of RESTART interviews for long-term unemployed adults in 1986, and survived until 1988, when it was replaced by Employment Training (ET). The need for a new programme for unemployed adults was outlined in the White Paper *Training for Employment*:[35]

> *First, many job seekers – particularly those who have been unemployed for six months or more – lack the skills to fill jobs our economy is generating. Second, many long-term unemployed people have lost touch with the job market, and lack motivation to take up a job, training or other opportunities. Third, there is evidence, particularly in the more prosperous parts of the country, that significant numbers of benefit claimants are not genuinely available for work.*

The Employment Training programme included one creative innovation in the key role given to the identification of training needs and the separation of guidance and needs analysis from the provision of training. But once again the programme was crippled by the inadequacy of the resources committed to training. However, the introduction of Employment Training was accompanied by a reduction in opportunities for unemployed people to take advantage of substantial part-time study opportunities in further education colleges. 21 Hour courses grew up to take advantage of a convention applied by the Department of Health and Social Security that enabled unemployed people to study for up to 21 hours a week and still to register as available for work and claim benefit. Student support for the majority of Access courses was financed by the 21 Hour Rule. The White Paper led to the introduction of new criteria to establish availability for work, particularly in areas where unemployment had fallen, with the effect that many people were unable to continue studying. Yet by November 1988, a new White Paper, *Employment for the 1990s*,[36] recognised that Britain needed to foster a learning workforce, and that demographic and industrial change meant that a million women would be needed in increasingly skilled jobs in the workforce, and that black people, older workers and people with disabilities would need to be recruited and persuaded to undertake training to become more skilled if Britain was to maintain its share as an industrial economy in increasingly international markets. Yet the main experience of contacting potential entrants to the labour market, giving people the confidence to embark on a programme of study or employment lies with adult education services, which have targeted exactly the groups that the Secretary of State identified in the White Paper. As the DES has adopted increasingly instrumental strategies in the later 1980s, however, adult education services have found their ability to undertake outreach work under consistent attack as public funding is withdrawn.

Throughout the 1980s government policy in respect of training was based on its faith in the efficacy of the market, and constrained by its larger commitment to the reduction of public expenditure. As the TUC observed: 'In no developed economy is the market vested with such power over training today [as in Britain and] nowhere else is it considered that individual investment decisions will provide the sort of trained workforce that a developed economy of the next century will need.'[37] *Training in Britain* showed that training opportunities are limited to some 30% of the population and, like post-compulsory education provision, recruits to training are likely to be middle class and to have enjoyed an extended initial education. It also showed that changing working patterns could make it more difficult to secure training for the whole workforce, since 'there is an increasing diversity in patterns of employment and employers concentrate training resources on their core staff'.[38]

For part-time workers, like part-time students, access to learning opportunities is likely to depend on the willingness of the state to provide funding support. Throughout the 1980s the government failed to meet that challenge.

Oddly, adult educators have found that large and enlightened enterprises have been more sympathetic than government to the need for adult learning opportunities. The Employee Development and Assistance Programme (EDAP) adopted by Ford and its trade unions in 1987 to provide workers with up to £200 to undertake a personal development learning project has been a huge success, with more than 50% of the workforce participating in courses ranging from German and computing, to golf and driving lessons, and an Open Learning programme on pub management. Rover have introduced a similar scheme, and firms like Lucas and Pedigree Pet Foods have comparable personal development opportunities at the heart of their human resource development strategies. Each recognises that investment in people is a key to economic success. In contexts where the supply of skilled labour is scarce, and where competitors are likely to match cash increases, the provision of learning opportunities can increase employees' satisfaction. More importantly, learning of all kinds encourages critical, flexible engagement with the task at hand, a key skill in a modern industrial workforce.[39]

The Education Reform Act 1988

It was striking in the light of this emerging consensus on Britain's industrial needs for flexible, skilled, learning adults that the Education Reform Act of 1988 should have had so little to say about adult learning, or about further education as a whole.[40] The debate and passage of the Act was accompanied by little effective lobbying on behalf of adult learners, except in Inner London, where the dangers to adult learning opportunities attendant on the winding-up of ILEA were predicted and rigorously debated in the Lords. As a sop to the London lobby the government agreed to fund centrally four centres of excellence in liberal education: the City Lit, Morley College, the Mary Ward Centre and England's oldest adult education institution, the Working Men's College. Whilst this was welcome, the neighbourhood adult education services which had been in the forefront of innovations and services to those communities traditionally under-represented were left to the tender mercies of the thirteen new local authorities established by the Act.

More broadly, the debate in Parliament made clear that a local education authority's duty to secure adequate facilities for further education included a duty to secure adequate adult education. The DES Circular issued a year after the passage of the Act to clarify local education authority responsibilities in planning and delegation schemes for the education of adults was significant in securing legislative recognition of the importance of adult learners.[41] The Circular recognised the plurality of adult education, and provided for broad programme funding areas: general adult education (an awkward term but less reverential than 'liberal', more purposeful than 'recreational'); second chance and basic education; and notably 'non-course provision', which included guidance, outreach work, drop-in centres and open learning. The Circular also recognised the importance of the voluntary sector by requiring local education authorities to consult voluntary providers. Whilst the Circular was permissive rather than prescriptive, it made clear government's view that efforts needed to be made to secure effective adult participation, and its recognition that time needed to be spent on 'non-course' activities, if accessibility was to be guaranteed.

At the same time UDACE advice to local education authorities on planning for the education of adults was making issues affecting adult learners less invisible.[42,43] There was a marked move to create community colleges, along the lines of the successful development in Newham, encompassing a wide diversity of strategies and the entire pattern of post-school education. The weight of discussion and decision-making deriving from the new vocationalism and the Education Reform Act concentrated on the links between adult learners and progression routes for work-related study. Yet forty-four authorities still organised the bulk of their adult education provision through services that combined youth services and adult education in community education. Through the last years of the 1980s little attention was paid to this less formal, process-centred dimension to adult learning.

It was, indeed, this work which suffered disproportionately when widespread charge-capping, or fear of charge-capping, accompanied the introduction of the Community Charge. Central government had reduced its contribution to local authority spending from 59% to 42% over the lifetime of Margaret Thatcher's governments and introduced systems of control of local government finance that had the effect of depleting expenditure across the board. Because adult education lacked protection as mandatory expenditure under statute the effect on general education of the introduction of the Community Charge was catastrophic in many, particularly urban, authorities. Barnsley stopped offering evening classes altogether, Manchester cut staff and budgets by 30% in 1990 and followed with more major cuts in 1991, Haringey cut its provision and budget by 50%, but it was in the former ILEA boroughs that the reduction in services to adult learners was most severe, with year-on-year reductions of up to half the very substantial budgets committed to adult learning.

Education and Training for the 21st Century

If political difficulties resulting from the method of financing local government provided the major motivation in the swathe of cuts at the turn of the 1990s, they were also a motivating force in the move to remove colleges from local education authorities in the 1991 White Paper *Education and Training for the 21st Century*.[44] The White Paper provides a logical conclusion to the evolution of DES policy affecting adult learners, and at the same time exposed the limitations of that policy.

The White Paper recognises the importance of adult learning to the work of further education colleges, and transfers responsibility from local education authorities to colleges for securing those aspects of further education central government wished to fund. It also limits the functions of publicly funded adult learning to measures which would lead to academic and vocational qualifications. Thus education for adults leading to A-Levels, AS Levels, GCSEs or to National Vocational Qualifications, access to higher education and access to higher levels of further education are secured; so are literacy and numeracy work, proficiency in English for speakers of other languages, and courses for adults with special educational needs. This narrowed curriculum is to be the beneficiary of all central funding for the education of adults.

Meanwhile, local education authorities are to retain the power to make provision of 'courses for the leisure interests of adults', and government recognises that such work 'can have a valuable social function'. No recognition is made in the White Paper of any other government purposes served by general provision for adults – no recognition of the learning needs of a rapidly ageing society, or of the role adult learning can play in prolonging active independent citizenship; no recognition of the place of general provision in supporting 'Care in the Community' policies; no recognition of the contribution local education services play in supporting active participation in arts and crafts. Because these issues are ignored, there is little consideration of the displaced costs on the exchequer resulting from weakening and closure of adult services. This policy thrust sits uneasily with the Employment Department's understanding that student purposes cannot simply be related to the provider's intentions, and that tomorrow's entrant to the labour force may be in a general adult education service today.

Prefigurative Forms of Adult Learning

If the market came early to adult education, its effects are still unravelling at the beginning of the 1990s. There can be no doubt that the key radical agenda setting of the 1980s came from a government wedded to the introduction of marketplace economics wherever possible. In adult education that led to pricing policies which have had the effect of narrowing participation. The effect of government policies has been a devastating reduction in provision for adult learners in Inner London, where adult education was best developed in the 1980s, and similar, smaller-scale reductions in other urban centres. They have led to some improvements in mobility through the post-school system – with widespread recognition of the importance of guidance, and at least lip-service paid to the importance of assessing and accrediting prior learning – and to a greater recognition of the needs of adult learners in colleges and polytechnics, if not always in universities. They have led to a re-assertion of the vocational/non-vocational divide, sentencing uncertificated work to the margins.

Overwhelmingly, the policies have led to a sustained attack on the idea that the common pursuit of knowledge for its own sake by groups of adult learners was a task which could make legitimate claims on the public purse. Work in adult education has, as a result, become more managerial: supervising small-scale mixed economies at the expense of curriculum innovation.

Of course, the government's agenda has not been implemented without contest. Perhaps the most striking development of an alternative role for adult learning opportunities in public policy was undertaken by the ILEA and the metropolitan authorities. Their commitment to equal opportunities policies led to the creative and imaginative curriculum developments outlined here. Curiously, given their political leadership, these authorities did little to address social class in their work. And, of course, central government used its greater powers to abolish this tier of local government altogether, and along with it much of the adult education provision generated.

With the abolition of metropolitan authorities and ILEA there was a clear loss of space for adult education workers who saw their role as working 'in and against the state', on behalf of the communities with which they worked, rather than the state which paid salaries. This has led to some loss of confidence among many adult educators committed to the empowerment of learners.

There is a serious danger of feeling that when people take away your budgets, they take away your soul. It is important to recognise that much of the work developed in the metropolitan authorities was evolved by negotiation between groups whose organisational forms did not depend on state patronage, and it is important to recognise that whilst in the short run there can be a loss of momentum with the withdrawal of funds, adults learn whether supported by the state or not. Among the most exciting developments of the 1980s have been the evolution of community-based learning projects that will use the resources of the state but are not dependent upon them. Castleford Women's Centre, Dowlais Women's Workshop, and Leicester's Belgrave Baheno are all women's organisations dedicated to learning which illustrate this as are the Pecket Well Literacy Centre, established by a group of adults with special needs, and the various groupings that make up the Federation of Worker Writers and Community Publishers. In a quite different context the success of the Ford EDAP, Rover Learning Business and others point to new alliances between private, public and not-for-profit bodies. In their different ways each illustrates prefigurative forms – ways of working which we may come to generalise in the future.

Despite the energy with which government sought to impose an agenda for the education of adults in the 1980s, it has remained true that the most creative responses to the complex aspirations of adult learners have been negotiated locally. Facing the 1990s, it is a strength of provision for adult learners, as well as a weakness, that it is so complex, various and plurally targeted. If people's aspirations were more narrowly constrained there would be no need for such a rich and textured pattern. After a decade in which the metaphor of the market has led the dance, we must look forward to the 1990s to the assertion by learners of their right to opportunities for learning – for work and for pleasure – that recognise their diversity and complexity.

References
1. *Hansard*, 25 July 1978, col 1400.
2. QueenSpark Rates Book Group, *Brighton on the Rocks: Monetarism and the local state*, Brighton: QueenSpark Books, 1982.
3. H.C. Wiltshire and G. Mee, *Structure and Performance in Adult Education*, Longman, 1978.
4. A.K. Stock, 'Into the 1980s', in *Yearbook of the National Institute of Adult Education, 1980–81*, Leicester: NIAE, 1980.
5. ibid.
6. Wiltshire and Mee, op.cit.
7. Stock, op.cit.
8. K.H. Lawson, *Save Adult Education Campaign Bulletin* 15, East Midlands Regional Institute of Adult Education, no date.
9. ibid.
10. *Adult Education* 52, 4, 1979.
11. A. Hemstedt and A. Tuckett, 'The Friends Centre Teach-In', *Adult Education* 54, 3, 1981.
12. Department of Education and Science, *Adult Education: A plan for development* (The Russell Report), HMSO, 1973.
13. P. Clyne, *The Disadvantaged Adult*, Longman, 1973.
14. J. Mace, *Working with Words*, Writers and Readers, 1979.

15. S. Nicholls and E. Murray, 'The unease of the outreach worker', in *The Aylesbury Estate: Report of an action research project*, Southwark Adult Education Institute, 1982.

16. Inner London Education Authority and National Institute of Adult Continuing Education, *Londoners Learning*, Leicester: NIACE, 1990.

17. Unit for the Development of Adult Continuing Education, *The Challenge of Change*, Leicester: UDACE, 1986.

18. Unit for the Development of Adult Continuing Education, *Open College Networks: Current developments and practice*, Leicester: UDACE, 1989.

19. Unit for the Development of Adult Continuing Education, *Developing Open College Networks*, Leicester: UDACE, 1990.

20. T. Alexander, *Value for People*, Clapham-Battersea Adult Education Institute, 1986.

21. Inner London Education Authority, *Changing Course*, ILEA, 1988.

22. *Hansard*, 16 January 1980, cols 1832–42.

23. B. Evans, *Radical Adult Education: A political critique*, Croom Helm, 1988.

24. Home Office, *Efficiency Scrutiny of Government Funding of the Voluntary Sector*, HMSO, 1990.

25. National Advisory Body for Public Sector Higher Education, *Strategy for Higher Education in the Late 1980s and Beyond*, NAB, 1984.

26. T. Bourner and M. Hamed, *Entry Qualifications and Degree Performance*, CNAA, 1987.

27. J.M. Williams, et al., *The Access Effect*, CNAA, 1989.

28. G. Melling and G. Stanton, 'Access to and through Further Education', in G. Parry and C. Wake (eds), *Access and Alternative Futures for Higher Education*, Hodder and Stoughton, 1990.

29. HMI, *The Contribution of Further and Higher Education to PICKUP*, HMSO, 1988.

30. A.G. Watts and E.G. Knasel, *Adult Education and the Curriculum: A manual for practitioners*, FEU/REPLAN, 1985.

31. National Institute of Adult Continuing Education, *Partnerships in Action*, Leicester: NIACE/REPLAN, 1989.

32. Manpower Services Commission, *A New Training Initiative*, Sheffield: MSC, 1981.

33. Manpower Services Commission, *Towards an Adult Training Strategy*, Sheffield: MSC, 1983.

34. Manpower Services Commission, *Annual Report 1983–84*, Sheffield: MSC, 1984.

35. Department of Employment, *Training for Jobs*, Cm 316, HMSO, 1988.

36. Department of Employment, *Employment for the 1990s*, Cm 540, HMSO, 1988.

37. Trades Union Congress, *Skills 2000*, TUC, 1989.

38. Training Agency, *Training in Britain, A Funding Study: The main report*, Department of Employment, 1989.

39. A. Tuckett, *Towards a Learning Workforce*, Leicester: NIACE, 1991.

40. Department of Education and Science, *Education Reform Act, 1988*, HMSO, 1988.

41. Department of Education and Science, *Circular 19/89: Adult Continuing Education and the Education Reform Act, 1988: Planning and delegation schemes*, HMSO, 1989.

42. Unit for the Development of Adult Continuing Education, *Adults and the Act*, Leicester: UDACE, 1988.

43. Unit for the Development of Adult Continuing Education, *Securing Adequate Facilities*, Leicester: UDACE, 1989.
44. Department of Education and Science and Employment Department Group, *Education and Training for the 21st Century*, Cm 1536, HMSO, 1991.

3

Constructing the Future: A postmodern agenda for adult education

SALLIE WESTWOOD

Postmodernism, the centre of lively debate in the social sciences and cultural criticism generally, has, so far, been largely ignored by adult education. But, this paper argues, the debates surrounding postmodernism have a special resonance for adult education and should be on the current agenda. The paper is necessarily tentative and exploratory, more in process than a finished statement, offering, in the spirit of the debates, an initial foray into an unfinished account of social, political and economic change. Underlying this as yet unfinished account is a philosophical intervention which seeks a deconstruction of foundationalism. This has profound implications for the social sciences, for politics and practice and, consequently, for adult education.

The term 'postmodern' is one attempt by writers like Lyotard[1] and Vattimo[2] to name the disjuncture between a former Western world marked by the modern, and the contemporary world, where profound changes in our forms of understanding, economic, social and political lives are evident. The 'modern' world of Europe was marked by the Enlightenment project which foregrounded 'rational man' (sic), scientific understanding and a linear view of progress towards a better world. It was from this background that the social sciences grew and Marxism developed, generating a world historic view of progress linked to the historical subject of the working class. It is against such foundationalism that both Vattimo and Lyotard argue. For Lyotard what we are witnessing in the postmodern world is the 'death of the grand narratives', the overarching explanatory theories, including Marxism, which have guided our politics and organised social change in the modern period. The underside of these modernist projects for progress, argues Lyotard, has been the rise of fascism and Stalinism, and the technologies of the death camps. The grand

44

narratives are now to be superseded by local narratives, a point to which I will return. Vattimo wants a new engagement for philosophical discourses which is to be generated out of an 'accomplished nihilism' which does not abdicate but provides instead a critical account, especially of the conditions generating alienation in Western cultures. We have to ask, however, whether there has indeed been a death of the grand narratives and whether a new nihilism offers us a way forward? These questions relate to the core area of the debate which centres around the significance of the changes underway. Are we living through a radical rupture between the modern and what we have come to call the postmodern, or is the latter a continuity of the former in a new guise? Clearly, times are changing rapidly and in Britain the current conjuncture has been named 'New Times', marked in Europe and the Soviet Union by the events of recent years which point to a rupture with Stalinism and the break up of the Soviet Empire. But the complexities of the moment also point to the contradictions. Current critics and writers are not uniformly suggesting that overnight a new economics, politics, literature and art has superseded the modern period, or that capitalism has disappeared. On the contrary, capitalism is yet again 'revolutionising the instruments of production' and generating profound changes. It is to a consideration of these changes and their characterisation that I now turn, taking three major areas: economics; politics; culture and identity.

Post-Fordism

The term post-Fordism is one attempt to name the processes of restructuring that have characterised capitalism in the post-Second World War period.[3] Urry and Lash[4] have used the term 'disorganised capitalism' as an alternative and to frame a somewhat wider analysis of these processes and to point to the separation between former modes of organising capitalist production and the present. The disjuncture to which they refer between past and present modes is captured in the reference to Ford, which in both the popular and academic literature speaks for a whole era of manufacturing based on mass markets for standardised products produced from assembly lines in large units with large workforces. This capitalist labour process was organised on the basis of a deskilled workforce controlled both by the assembly line itself and by a centralised management structure using Taylorist work study techniques. The production processes were not the preserve of the West but were also part of the socialist economies and the newly developing nations. Working conditions generated a male world of labour which was highly organised through the trade union movement and a shopfloor culture which was itself subversive, generating its own norms, values and rituals from within the world of labour. Although women have consistently been part of the world of labour they were often absent from the union and party discourses which organised resistance and generated a politics of production. Thus, the suggestion that Fordism has been fractured by restructuring has major implications for the models of politics which were generated around labour and the contradictions between capital and labour writ large by Fordism itself.

The new model of production for what I would call 'reorganised' rather than 'disorganised' capitalism is the model of flexible specialisation known globally through Toyota and Benetton, where the move is away from concentrated, large-scale production with a large workforce onsite. Instead, production of commodities is generated through a network of small firms that supply a part in the operation overall and that are co-ordinated through the use of computer technologies and decentralised management. Core workers are flexible, highly trained and enjoy secure employment and high rewards, while, at the same time, there is a growing sector of peripheral workers who are very often women, migrants and black workers whose work is casualised and their working lives are marked by insecurity, low pay and lack of unionisation.

Operations can be global, with one commodity manufactured around the world in its component parts and assembled wherever conditions for capital are most advantageous. The processes of globalisation are an essential part of post-Fordism. In Britain the retailing and distribution of goods has already been revolutionised by computer technologies which allow computerised stock control and warehousing. The processes at work mean that fewer workers are now employed in the manufacturing sector and a higher proportion in services. In Britain three-fifths of workers work in services. Coupled with this shift is the move to part-time employment, which now accounts for one in four jobs in Britain, and the increasing feminisation of the workforce. Estimates suggest that 90 per cent of new jobs in Britain in the next few years will be taken by women. Currently, women account for 50 per cent of the workforce but it is noteworthy that black women are more likely to be in full-time employment and that the shift to part-time working does not satisfy their demands for full-time employment. Part-time employment has increased alongside homeworking, which involves many women in poorly paid forms of manufacturing within the domestic unit, especially in the clothing industry, which has shifted away from factory production and towards small units and the home.[5] Alongside these changes has been the rise in self-employment, especially among Asians in Britain, which has been, in part, a consequence of racism in employment and restructuring in manufacturing. Many of these small businesses operate at the margins and there is a very high rate of failure despite the 'rags to riches' stories favoured by the popular press.

The changes in production and employment are not, however, uniform; the success of McDonalds, a monument to the Fordism of food, alerts us to the contradictory tendencies. These contradictions have been central to the restructuring of the public sector in Britain, where Fordist management styles are aligned with market forces as a model for the future development of education, health and social services. Educators in Britain are being inducted into a language of performance indicators and competency measures, of efficiency and through-put which is generating a sort of measured day work for education.

Post-Fordism has profound implications for adult education in a number of related ways. Adult education in Britain has never been a simple unit; it has been contested terrain and some part of it has allied itself closely and has deep historical roots in the Labour movement and its struggles. Adult education has worked with the trade union movement on shop stewards' programmes and on wider educational ventures that have connected with the cultures and programmes of workers. The changes in production processes, however, throw this work into sharp relief and raise some fundamental questions about the nature of vocational education as well. Government has made major interventions into training programmes through the Training Agency, which has centralised much of this work and controlled it accordingly. The new model is one of decentralisation through the Training and Enterprise Councils that will contract educational establishments and training companies to provide programmes. The TECs are controlled by employers on a regional basis and have a low level of involvement by unions and workers. Workers, however, need to have a voice in the training that they will receive and a means whereby they can articulate the demands that they have for training in the post-Fordist era.

The government view of an employer-led training initiative cuts across the optimistic account of flexible specialisation which sees in the new methods of working and local workplaces moves towards new forms of ownership and control for workers and thereby higher rates of participation, with consequences for a new democratisation of working lives. Adult education, with its historical links and expertise in trade union education, would be well placed to intervene in the new processes of democratisation and worker participation but, thus far, its expertise has been marginalised by the new training initiatives.

Production is one side of the equation while consumption is the other. Fordism produced a standardised product for a mass market, as does McDonalds. But while globalisation carries McDonalds around the world, mass markets are simultaneously fractured and capitalist firms face a new structure of demand which segments and differentiates markets. The evidence for this is in every High Street and shopping centre in Britain, where companies like the ill-fated Next, for example, appear as retail outlets with monotonous regularity, but within this each of the shops serves a different market segment, offering a 'home' to different sets of consumers. The designer eighties were a reaction to standardisation and uniformity. Consumers with purchasing power demanded and received consumption goods that marked their status and power. This, of course, is not new; hand-made shirts and Saville Row suits have always differentiated a specific section of consumers but the attempt to reproduce this for a larger market was enormously successful in the eighties. At the same time the gap between those with purchasing power and those without grew steadily through the decade, fuelled by the processes of restructuring that produced record levels of unemployment. Manufacturers looked to the generation of markets and market niches for an increasingly wide range of products and marketing took on a new sophistication. The economic, class-based categories of previous marketing strategies were interwoven with life-style categories which fractured the class categories and produced the now well-known acronyms YUPPIES and DINKIES. In the nineties, grey power and the 'fifty something' generation are the targets of new sales pitches related to an anthropology of life-style which transforms the population of Britain into a complex style map and citizens into consumers. This has generated a new politics of consumption and new meanings for identities called forth through specific consumption patterns.

Mainstream British adult education has constructed an account of itself in which the market is crucial. The field abounds with discourses on the consumer- and market-led nature of adult education courses within the language of 'needs' and 'provision'. This has had major implications for the type of research done in adult education which has concentrated on a class-based map of the consumers, not surprising, given the saliency of class in Britain. But any account of class structure needs to be articulated with 'race' and gender formation. The recent ILEA/NIACE survey, *Londoners Learning*, moves this forward by its attention to gender and ethnicity and the attempt to situate consumers within a view of a 'learning culture'.[6] Generally, however, adult education has adopted a minimalist approach to marketing the field and an imperialist approach to the development of new sectors. By this I mean the ways in which 'the elderly' or 'ethnic minorities' have entered adult education discourses as homogenous entities and the objects of provisions, rather than as fractured groupings with both distinctive and common demands. Adult education could usefully develop an interest in the anthropology of life-styles in Britain because the consumption of cultural commodities is an intrinsic part of this and the evident variety of 'genres' of consumption has implications for adult education. This is not to ignore the intensive community-based development work done as part of adult education in which attention is focused on specific local cultures. What is required is for this type of analysis and practice to feed into the mainstream through a reconstructed view of adult education as a cultural field, one which is itself very diverse and which faces an increasingly diverse series of discrete and interacting consumer demands. Yet is the language of consumption empowering for adult education, or a denial of the relationship between education and culture? The possibility exists for adult education to reconstruct the interface between cultural consumption and education in order to engage with the new 'politics of consumption'.

The Politics of Postmodernism

The new phase of capitalist development, away from Fordist production methods, has profound implications for politics and especially for the politics of the Left, traditionally bound to production and the male, white working class. In another language, it is in the terrain of politics that the move away from the 'grand narratives' has most impact, most importantly in relation to Marxist inspired politics where the grand narrative of class struggle and the defeat of exploitation and alienation through socialism has provided an agenda for political analysis and action throughout the twentieth century. Political events in Europe have foregrounded the socialist agenda during recent years and given new momentum to debates already underway in the Communist parties of Europe. That the debates were already in train alerts us to the ways in which the Left has sought to understand the demise of organised class politics in the post-68 era through a shift away from Leninist analysis and towards a Gramscian account which foregrounds a politics of civil society and cultural leadership.[7] Writers like Callinicos[8] dispute this, holding fast to a revolutionary Marxism that is not in need of reconstruction. For Callinicos, like other critics, there are no 'New Times' and the attempt to generate them is merely a route out of the impasse generated by the failure of Left intellectuals to engage with revolutionary politics. 'New Times' offers a way out of the impasse, but critics have characterised it as little more than 'designer socialism' and a complement to the possessive individualism of the Thatcher years in Britain.

Postmodern politics is a politics in formation, concerned as much with process as with ends and located, for Lyotard, with local narratives. At the same time it is clear that these local narratives often have core connections with global concerns – green issues are a prime example of this. It is a politics prefigured by the decline of class politics and the rise of the 'new social movements' for peace, women's liberation, racial justice, gay liberation and green issues.[9] Feminism, anti-racism and environmental issues have given a new meaning to single issue, pressure group politics that have been recast in the last twenty years. This is, in part, a consequence of economic restructuring and the profound impact it has had on the labour movement, but it is also part of a different political vision and form of understanding which is bound up with questions of identity and the self. The view from feminism that 'the personal is political' prefigured the current emphasis, but in other ways feminism held fast to a politics organised around an essentialist view of 'woman' that privileged certain voices and marginalised others, especially those of black women. The debates within feminism have fractured a unitary view but this does not necessarily mean a collapse into local narratives. Fraser and Nicholson[10] point to the need for meta-narratives and comment:

> *Whereas some women have common interests and face common enemies, such commonalities are by no means universal; rather they are interlaced with differences, even with conflicts. This, then is a practice made up of a patchwork of overlapping alliances, not one circumscribable by an essential definition. One might best speak of it in the plural as the practice of 'feminisms'. Thus, commonality and difference speak simultaneously and cannot be bound to a unitary view of women or an overarching, trans-historical theory of patriarchy.*

A diverse, shifting politics of difference is foregrounded by the postmodern account and highlighted by the current events in Europe, where national and ethnic identities have exploded, once again, into the political area. It is a contradictory politics, calling forth political identities from ethnic identifications which have been submerged in the post-war period but also generating revived chauvinisms and racisms formed through the essentialist discourses postmodernism seeks to deconstruct. Potentially, it combines a liberatory discourse around difference and the celebration of cultural and ethnic diversities with a reactionary and dangerous exclusivity. Thus, in Britain, British identity is currently the focus of debate, generating a contestation which confronts the hegemony of Englishness with a multi-racial population calling forth British identities both through the historical legacy of Empire and the contemporary situation in Britain. And it is not just that black people will be British; the complexities of what it means to be black in British society have been thrown into sharp relief by the protests against Salman Rushdie and *The Satanic Verses*. British Muslims have asserted a Muslim identity and organised around it and made claims against the state for full citizenship rights under the law through their presence on the streets and the legal battles in which they are engaged. The politics of difference is central to the contested terrain of British identity.

Citizenship has been returned to the political agenda by both Right and Left. In Britain Thatcherism has generated a view of the active citizen located with a new politics of consumption which effectively disenfranchises the impoverished sections of a society in which the gap between rich and poor has widened in the last decade. The Left has responded with a call for citizenship constructed through difference, in which feminist and anti-racist claims have a role[11] and in which the hegemony of the white English man is fractured. This is articulated with a view of collective consumption in which consumer interests and power are used to produce more sensitive and high quality public services accountable to consumers. The notion that to be a 'consumer' rather than a 'client' is empowering links the arena of welfare to the broader changes in the economy and the structure of demand. The magazine *New Consumer* asserts: '*New Consumer* gives you the power to make choices' – but in relation to what? The politics of consumption is a precarious strategy for the Left. Consumer boycotts, for example, have a long history as part of the attempt to control multinationals and register a political protest in relation to South Africa, but this type of action has been allied with other forms and is often, and correctly, conceived as solidarity work rather than a form of autonomous political action. A politics of consumption is one thing, to collapse politics into consumption is potentially a domestication, a 'seduction'.[12]

The debates around citizenship and the articulation between citizenship, socialism and forms of democracy have been given a powerful impetus by events in Europe and the Soviet Union, where the move to representative democracy has called up earlier political cultures with the consequence that the outcomes across Europe are distinctive. This diversity is an essential part of the 'New Europe' and the new politics with which the 'Old Europe' must now engage. Central to this is a politics of difference generated from the ethnic diversity of Europe and its imperial days which have multiplied ethnic identities throughout Europe. The debate on English ethnicity is now given context by this and it is one in which the English, so ready to construct 'Otherness' in subject populations, now confront their own 'Otherness'. It is to be hoped that from this an English ethnicity can be constructed which has a place amid many other ethnicities, but that it is not privileged.

Adult education in Britain has a long history of engagement with the issue of citizenship but, like the workers education to which it was often allied, it has been located with the labour movement and a version of citizenship that ignored difference. 'New Times' requires a radical revision of this account, one that generates discourses within the context of a British identity that is shifting terrain. Political education more generally has to attend to the articulation between local narratives and global concerns and to the ways in which the links between the specific and the general are made and understood. [13] The new social movements, with their emphasis on process, have in themselves been educative in ways with which adult education is well placed to connect, as it did in relation to the community politics of the seventies. Ultimately, and more profoundly, to enter into an engagement with a postmodern naming of the world is to enter the political arena because, as Boyne and Rattansi make clear:[14]

> *One common theme can be found across all the writings concerned with delineating the new postmodern perspective. This common theme is that postmodernism is, in the broadest sense, 'political'. Through its entire range, postmodernist discourse presents questions about how social relations should be organised and lived, about the social possibilities of our age, and about the social visions it is desirable to underwrite in the postmodern epoch.*

Culture and Identity

The new movements in art, architecture, literature, music and film have been central to the landscape of postmodernism and the subjects of heated public debates. The move is away from the debates about form and function that framed so much of modernist cultural practice and towards a deconstructionist art practice which uses pastiche, irony and sometimes playfulness, drawing on the past in eclectic ways which some would argue so decontextualises history that it is merely plunder. Films like *Diva*, *Blue Velvet* or *Repo Man* work with the forms of previous eras, away from narrative accounts and operate at a variety of levels simultaneously. Some black film-makers and feminist artists have embraced the new ways of seeing as providing a space away from notions of 'positive images', thereby freeing themselves in order to offer more fully the complexities of the experience of black people and women. Artists like Barbara Kruger and black photographers like David Bailey point to the ways in which images are constructed and the multiple readings available. In this their work shares the central themes of postmodernist cultural practices. The first and major premise is the breaking down of the barriers constructed between 'Art' and popular culture. Secondly, the objective is to deconstruct the barriers between different art forms. Thus, Barbara Kruger's work uses photographs, some within the conventions of advertising, and brings together visual images with text that generate a critique of sexism and consumerism in Western societies. Not unlike the earlier movements of the twentieth century, DaDa and Surrealism, the new movement seeks to disturb taken-for-granted worlds and to shift the line between fantasy and reality. There is no nostalgia and sentiment for the past but a revelry in the new and in the coming together of cultural variety.

The debates in architecture, not surprisingly, have been some of the most public, due to the visibility of the changes in our cityscapes marked by the shift away from the glass and steel towers to the decorative multivalent buildings of the last decade. Postmodern architecture begins from a notion that there cannot be one reading of a building, one way in which people will relate to the built environment. The point, therefore, is to build with ambivalence and contradiction, allowing and encouraging a multiplicity of readings. This is an eclectic architecture bringing together styles and materials that are juxtaposed rather than complementary, on a much smaller scale than the high-rise world of the post-war period. The eclecticism of the current architecture provides a series of signs that require decoding, not once but often twice. Without this 'double coding' the architecture may appear chaotic, a mishmash of tasteless eclecticism without form or referents, a disunity compared with the geometric simplicity of modernist buildings. The point, however, is to fracture the unity that the building may better relate to the context and to the people who will use and view the building. Jencks, [15] an enthusiastic supporter of postmodern architecture, underlines the view that architecture has to communicate and only by so doing will it overcome the elitism of the earlier eras.

While architecture shifts scale and seeks connections with a local context and other historical and cultural traditions this is mirrored in cultural consumption in contemporary cities. Food, music, clothes are an intercultural and interethnic admixture from across the globe. It could be argued that this is the worst of cultural imperialism, which sells disconnected elements of cultures to mindless consumers. But such a view would miss the dynamic of cultural forms. The consumer's relationship is certainly fleeting and mediated by the cash nexus but it does not, necessarily, end with the commodification of cultures, or parts of cultures and may incorporate more progressive elements. The politicisation of popular culture has been shown by the ways in which popular music has been woven together in events like Band-Aid and the celebration of Nelson Mandela and the ANC. The medium of television has given these events a global immediacy which has linked cultural consumption to politics concerned with global issues. Popular culture has, therefore, many voices and recent analyses of the most popular of cultural products, like soap operas, have tried to connect with the multiplicity of meanings produced. Soap operas do not operate with a single closed narrative but with contradictions in an open narrative that makes many readings possible. They offer viewers particular pleasures which cannot be discounted. Attempts within television, like Dennis Potter's *Black Eyes*, are a move away from narrative and a coming together of fantasies interwoven in complex and critical ways. Thus, we begin to read popular culture and its

pleasures differently and in 'New Times' are much less dismissive of the politics
of culture, offering instead a centrality to struggles around representations and
within cultural politics.

Adult education can be viewed as a cultural field and should, therefore,
relate to the current politics of culture. This was, of course, central to the
views brought to adult education by Raymond Williams, and many adult
educators have been deeply populist in orientation. 'New Times' means,
however, a more cross-cultural and global view and adult education needs
to examine the curricula with which it works and the ways in which in
the field is ethnocentric. To engage with postmodern accounts of culture
also means engaging politically with the knowledge/power complex. Much
of our current understanding of cultural politics has been informed by the
work of Gramsci and attention has been focused on the ways in which work
in adult education can be counter-hegemonic and empowering, and this focus
provides a background to a new engagement with cultural consumption. This
would profoundly alter the way in which adult education in Britain constructs
an image of itself.

The issues of consumption and image return us to the politics of identity
which have been foregrounded within postmodern debates. This has given a
new meaning to the politics of subjectivities framed by a post-structuralist
language which decentres subjectivity and the self. The coherent unified subject
of earlier discourses is replaced by a shifting and contradictory collection of
'multiple selves'[16] called forth by a multiplicity of discourses, and this view
has profound implications for adult education practice. Adult education has
claimed specificity through its students who are adults, but, apart from notions
of multiple roles and stages in adult lives, little attention has been given to the
ways in which 'the adult' is constructed and positioned in adult education
discourses. The new terrain of the self has major implications for the ways
in which we view the adult as learner and the process of learning itself. It
leads to a re-examination of the power/knowledge complex in adult education
and to an excavation of the discourses which construct adult education and
the ways in which subjects are positioned within these discourses as the
subject/objects of knowledge. That subjects come into adult education with
class, gender, ethnic, regional, economic, political identities is not unknown in
adult education and the variety and diversity of programmes on offer speaks to
this multiplicity of selves. The regional and local focus of much adult education
work also means that adult educators would suggest that although multiple
selves may, indeed, be shifting and contradictory they are not ahistorical
but are placed in histories, locales, languages and cultures which generate
commonalities and shared meanings which also have a bearing upon adult
education practice and the processes of education more widely. The decentred

view of the subject, however, allows adult education to look anew at 'the adult' and 'the learner' in ways which will enhance our understandings of learning processes.

Not Yet Concluded

The foregoing discussion suggests that adult education is peculiarly well placed to engage with the account of the present conjuncture as postmodern. The issues that have been foregrounded by the debates around economics, politics, culture and identity have a special resonance with a field which has, throughout its history, been contested terrain. Some part of adult education has, historically, been allied with a vision of the emancipation of the working class. But the view of the changing nature of production relations characterised as post-Fordist presents a new landscape of industrial relations and the role of workers within this which can only partly be related to a labour movement conceived in terms of white male workers. Similarly, the foregrounding of citizenship reiterates a theme with a long history in adult education, but this theme has been reworked in relation to the events in Europe and the Soviet Union and in relation to a new politics of difference. But it is clear that the emphasis on difference can too easily assume an equivalence which ignores extant power relations. However, this does have major implications for the ways in which adult education addresses the issue of citizenship and how it can work with difference rather than against it. Similarly, the politics of consumption and the language of consumers offers adult education new ways with which to work through the intersection of culture, education and consumption in relation to the growing diversity of adult education in Britain. This represents the possibility of a reframing of adult education which integrates the past with the present and provides a new impetus for work in the coming decade. Both culture and consumption have come together in a new politics of subjectivities which focus attention on a decentred view of the subject and novel ways of theorising the adult and the learner. This is a profound shift which will open up new ways of understanding learning processes within the field and will have major implications for practice. Radical adult education has, historically, worked at the interface of economics, politics and cultures, often in the spaces opened up by this intersection. It is precisely at this interface that the language of 'New Times' makes its intervention, and why it has such powerful resonances for adult education.

References
1. J.-F. Lyotard, *The Postmodern Conditions: a Report on Knowledge*, Minnesota: University of Minnesota Press, 1984.

2. G. Vattimo, *The End of Modernity: Nihilism and Hermeneutics in Post-Modern Culture*, Cambridge: Polity Press, 1988.

3. R. Murray, 'Life after Henry (Ford)', *Marxism Today* October 1988.

4. J. Urry and S. Lash, *The End of Organised Capitalism*, Cambridge: Polity Press, 1987.

5. A. Phizacklea, 'Minority women and economic restructuring: the case of Britain and the Federal Republic of Germany', *Work, Employment and Society* 1, 3, 1987, pp 309–325.

6. Inner London Education Authority and National Institute of Adult Continuing Education, *Londoners Learning*, Leicester: NIACE, 1990.

7. N. Bobbio, 'Gramsci and the concept of civil society' in J. Keane (ed.), *Civil Society and the State*, Verso, 1988, pp 73–100.

8. A. Callinicos, *Against Postmodernism*, Cambridge: Polity Press, 1990.

9. A. Melucci, *Nomads of the Present: Social Movements and Individual Needs in Contemporary Society*, Hutchinson Radius, 1989.

10. N. Fraser and L. Nicholson, 'Social criticism without philosophy: an encounter between feminism and postmodernism', *Theory, Culture and Society* 5, 2–3, 1988, pp 373–94.

11. S. Hall and D. Held, 'Left and rights', *Marxism Today* June 1989.

12. Z. Bauman, 'Is there a postmodern sociology?', *Theory, Culture and Society* 5, 2–3, 1988, pp 217–238.

13. M. Lichtner, 'Political education of adults: specific instances and the general view', *Studies in the Education of Adults* 22, 1, 1990, pp 3–13.

14. R. Boyne and A. Rattansi, 'The theory and politics of postmodernism: by way of an introduction' in R. Boyne and A. Rattansi (eds), *Postmodernism and Society*, Macmillan, 1990, pp 1–45.

15. C. Jencks, *The Language of Post-Modern Architecture*, Academy Editions, 1984.

16. S. Hall, 'Brave new world', *Marxism Today* October 1988.

This article is an edited version of a paper first given at a seminar at the Centro Europeo dell'Educazione, Frascati, in May 1990.

Part II

Innocence and After: The Seventies

4

Community Adult Education

T. LOVETT

(Studies in Adult Education, 3, 1971.)

[Mr Lovett is a WEA organising tutor working as one of the Educational Priority Area team in a poor area of central Liverpool. This article is a personal report on his first fourteen months' work, and should be read in conjunction with Mr Keith Jackson's article in our last issue.]

My work to date has convinced me that there is a huge need and potential for adult education provision for working-class communities if the adult education movement in this country is prepared to remove its shackles and adopt a radically new approach. Numerous writers in recent years have urged the responsible bodies to adopt such an approach, but unfortunately most of these writers have been concerned with the *why* rather than the *how*. The key to the situation, I believe, is that adult education must be seen, not simply as classes and discussions for the adult members of the community, but rather as an integral part of a whole series of activities – sponsored by government, the local authority, voluntary agencies, churches, residents' groups – which are community-based and concerned with the total community. This is not to say that adult education is indistinguishable from these community activities, but in order to succeed it must work very closely with them. This often means adopting a very flexible approach in which adult education fills a number of different but related roles. The roles I see are six, namely:

(1) Adult education cum community development.
(2) Adult education as a resource in community development.
(3) Adult education as an aid to parents and schools.
(4) Adult education as a forum for discussing personal, moral, and social problems.
(5) Adult education as an extension of recreation and entertainment.
(6) Adult education as a counselling service for individuals and groups.

All these roles can be illustrated from my Liverpool experience.

Adult Education cum Community Development

Community development or community action is the only practical course
which an adult educationist can adopt in certain situations when working
with some communities in an Educational Priority Area. He should even be
prepared to see, and if necessary encourage, other slightly more traditional
adult educational situations to develop in this direction if the participants
show some desire to move from the theoretical to the practical. Sometimes
the practical can lead on to a slightly more formal type of adult education,
and vice versa. On other occasions the process can go through three stages, i.e.
discussion, practice, discussion.

An example of this is my work with residents in the Salisbury Centre.[1]
Here I encouraged the residents to make use of a disused handicraft centre
as a meeting place for informal discussions. They saw the possibilities of the
building as a youth and community centre and succeeded in convincing the
local authority that they should be given the lease. This took place over a
period of nine months during which time the residents concerned organised
a committee to look after their affairs, met local councillors to discuss their
problems, and catered for the young people in the area. Here was an example
of learning through doing, acquiring new skills and knowledge. Now the
residents are keen to provide some form of adult education in the centre and
they look to me to help. An application has been made for £5,000 from the
Urban Aid Programme and the hope is that the building will become a fully
equipped community and youth centre with an adult education bias.

Another example of a 'learning through doing' situation is the Shelter Neighbourhood Action Plan in the Granby area of Liverpool 8. Here the residents
were assisted by the SNAP team in setting up 'task forces' to discuss *their*
solutions to a wide variety of problems to do with education, housing, traffic,
etc. The task forces met corporation officials and other outside experts so that
they could learn their views. This was not a simulated situation. The SNAP
team were intent on getting the residents to use the provisions of the 1969
Housing Act, both to renovate their own properties and to bring pressure
on the corporation to make the whole area a general improvement area, with
a consequent inflow of local authority finance. In the event they succeeded.
In this case I was responsible for setting up the participation structure, for
liaison with the various task forces, and for translating complicated town
planning jargon into layman's language. This was a different situation from
that in Salisbury Street. Another body, a voluntary agency concerned with
housing, was responsible for the initiative in encouraging the residents to take
some practical steps towards solving their problems. I was a member of that

team, helping in a practical way by offering the advice and assistance of one who saw the project as an exercise in adult learning.

I have two other exercises planned. One is an attempt to help a group of mothers to set up a claimants' union. Originally we met as an informal discussion group linked to a bingo session. However, I soon discovered that most of the mothers were either separated or divorced and claiming some sort of welfare benefit. They spent a lot of time talking about the problems associated with claiming benefits and asking for my views and assistance. From these discussions arose the suggestion to form a branch of the claimants' union. The other exercise is concerned with helping local residents establish a credit union, i.e. to pool their financial resources and set up a loan fund, so that their members can avoid the moneylender or hire-purchase charges.[2] Such exercises can be exciting experiments in adult education, with people learning to deal with real, immediate problems in a practical way, picking up essential skills and items of information as they go along. To seek a formal structure and treat such groups as 'classes' is to impose middle-class standards in working-class situations, and in most instances, at least in EPAs, such efforts will lead to failure and alienation.

Adult Education as a Resource for Community Development

Even when the adult educator is less directly involved in community development he can still make his skills available as a resource to community groups. For instance, when the task forces in SNAP completed their work and combined into a SNAP residents' group I was able to offer my advice as an adult educationist on how best to tackle the director of housing. We spent two meetings discussing what points to raise, how to raise them and who was to raise them. My involvement in the earlier stages of the project made my acceptance by the residents at this stage relatively easy. I was able to point to certain deficiencies in their approach based on shared experience and knowledge. My hope is that at a future stage the residents will become involved in a series of discussions on the practical problems of running a committee. At the moment they are not ready to participate in anything so formal.

However, with another residents' group which has been functioning for some time, I have been able to organise a short course on committee procedure. I have also had success in establishing discussions for residents operating advice centres, and I am negotiating with youth leaders in the area on the organisation of a training course for local residents who are helping in various youth clubs and centres.

Much of this type of work depends on the ability to recognise the occasion when adult education can be of assistance. Most residents' groups do not realise that many of their problems are in fact educational and that educational assistance is something they can call upon. It is necessary, therefore, to attend meetings of residents to make oneself known and accepted so that when the occasion arises such assistance can be offered. For instance, at a recent meeting of a local community council, a local government publication was referred to by the chairman. I was able to convince the residents that it would be profitable to set up a sub-committee to have a look at the document with my assistance – and then to offer their views to the local authority.

It is essential that all these efforts should be kept initially on an informal and *ad hoc* basis. In Liverpool the unskilled and semi-skilled working classes have borne the brunt of the redevelopment process and this has added to their misfortunes by disrupting community life. Thus in the Liverpool EPA there are no working-class 'communities' in the old sense of the word, but merely individuals seeking to come to terms with a new environment. In such a situation community groups serve not just as organisations to voice residents' complaints but as a social binding force. The act of coming together is itself a step forward in engendering a new sense of community. Formal 'courses', on the other hand, are impracticable and self-defeating. This is not to say that such courses will not be accepted at a later stage in the development of community groups.

Adult Education as an Aid to Parents and Schools

When I first took up this post it was felt that this could be the most profitable field of development for adult education. Plowden had emphasised the importance of parental interest in the child's development at school and my secondment to the Liverpool EPA was seen as an opportunity to follow up the Plowden recommendations on home-school links and involvement of parents in the educational process. This has not proved easy.

So far, I have had only partial success in encouraging parents to take part in discussions about their children's education. One residents' association did begin a series of informal discussions on 'Children and their Education', designed to inform parents of the changes now taking place in the school curriculum and methods, but the range of discussion was soon widened to include other topics of general interest. At one school I succeeded in getting some of the mothers to agree to a joint project with the children on the history of the district but it fell through owing to lack of support.

It is difficult to account for this 'apparent' lack of interest but I believe there are a number of possible explanations:

(i) The process of explaining modern school subjects to parents repeats the mistake made with the children, i.e. using a middle-class technique to help solve a working-class problem. Professor Bernstein in a recent lecture in Liverpool made this very point and expressed his pessimism about such methods in enlisting parental support.[3] My experience would lead me to agree with him.

(ii) The situation in the Liverpool EPA is such that what concerns parents most is the lack of play facilities for children. Hence they are often full of praise for the schools but critical of the local authority for its shortsightedness in not making more provision for children after school hours and during the holidays. This is a pressing problem for many families in the area, especially since it would appear that the break-up of the older communities has destroyed the ability of children to organise their own play in the streets. Street games in working-class communities meant that children were occupied without parental involvement. Parents did not need to think of how they could provide for their children's leisure hours – the street provided for them.

Today it is necessary to think of what to do for the children and many community groups in Liverpool have sprung up because of an interest in solving this particular problem. Thus, I found myself during the summer of 1970 organising a summer play scheme with the emphasis on parental involvement.[4] I enlisted the support of some students from a local college of education and filled the Salisbury Centre with a wide range of educational toys and games. The idea was to interest the parents in the sort of activities which would be of educational benefit to their children. I was not wholly successful but with my encouragement the parents did organise a series of bus trips to places of interest, as well as teaching the children how to swim and organising a football competition. It was the first time parents in the area had organised anything of this nature.

If parents in an EPA are to take a more active interest in education then I believe it is necessary to get parents to discuss what the educational system is about. What is education for? What sort of education do their children receive? What does it equip them for? Is there the possibility of another criterion for judging educational competence? What part can they play in such a dialogue? Of course these are very abstract questions but I hope that two projects I have in hand may wed the need for practical work with the possibility of a discussion of certain concepts to do with education. They are:

(i) In co-operation with a neighbouring community arts centre I am producing an 'EPA Show' using game-playing techniques. This centre is specially concerned to extend into higher and adult education something of that game-playing activity – a synthesis of education, enjoyment, discovery and creativity – which has already been successful in some of our primary schools. The aim is to promote increased awareness of social problems and to encourage discussion, often between professionals in the social service field and the people they are trying to help. The centre has already gained some considerable experience in this type of work and it is hoped to use this experience in a 'show' aimed at parents and concerned with the problem of education in an EPA. This will be an exercise bringing together a number of bodies engaged in educational and community work in Liverpool and it is hoped that ways and means can subsequently be found to make use of the game-playing technique in more normal adult education situations.[5]

(ii) The kit on education supplied by the Humanities Curriculum Project for senior pupils in secondary modern schools can, I feel, be used with some EPA adult groups. Discussion can often become disoriented even with a good tutor and can be greatly helped by 'evidence' such as the kit on education provides, i.e. extracts from newspapers, books, poems, songs, tape-recordings, film material, photographs.[6]

These two projects may well prove to be the most exciting and valuable experiments to be carried out in the field of home-school education in the EPA.

Adult Education as a Forum for discussing Personal, Moral and Social Problems

This aspect of community adult education in the Liverpool EPA has proved extremely successful, especially with women. For example, a group of young mothers undertook a series of discussion under my direction on 'The Community and the Outsider', the object of which was to examine the role of the various groups regarded as being outside the community, e.g. drug addicts and alcoholics. With other groups I drew up a list of topics – talking points for adults – based on the sort of problems often discussed in the national press and TV, e.g. abortion, teenagers, hanging, divorce, the permissive society, etc. The group then chose six or seven topics. Not surprisingly most of the groups chose subjects of personal concern, and with the help of some films lively discussions ensued. The discussions were in most instances seen as an extension of the social activities of the group, so that one week they had bingo, another week a discussion. Sometimes the two were associated in the same session.

Informality is the keynote. In one group held in a local school – during school hours – the mothers bring their younger children. The success of these discussions bears out the point made by the Marriage Guidance Council in its evidence to the Russell Committee,[7] i.e. that there is a real need for a forum to enable adults to discuss their problems, fears and anxieties, in a society where values are changing and most institutions are undergoing a period of reassessment.

I am also engaged in writing a number of scripts for Radio Merseyside on the general theme 'You and Authority'. The purpose of these fifteen-minute programmes is to have a look at the institutions which at one time gave a certain sense of stability to working-class communities, i.e. the family, the neighbourhood, the church and the school. The programmes are intended as a stimulus for discussion groups in the EPA. They will avoid too much talk and will emphasise drama. Thus the first programme on 'The Family' will open with a dramatic recreation of family life two or three generations ago, and then go on to collect views and opinions from some families in Liverpool.

The points I would like to emphasise about these groups are:

(i) They responded positively to my suggestions because I emphasised the informality of the proceedings and the link with existing social activities.

(ii) The educational element was not over-stressed. My experience has shown that this is often a deterrent.

(iii) The personal relationship between 'tutor' and 'class' is extremely important. The ability to get on with people, to communicate on a personal level is essential.

(iv) Tutors must accept that one activity will flow into another, and must be willing to become involved in other activities connected with the group, e.g. helping with a Christmas pantomime or organising a bazaar.

Adult Education as an Extension of Recreation and Entertainment

Adult education has, it would appear, an image of seriousness for many working-class adults which is at variance with their life-style, in which the emphasis is on informality and enjoyment. With this in mind I decided to take adult education into the social focal point of working-class community, i.e. the local pub. I used a *Sunday Mirror* type approach, emphasising the sensational aspects of the themes chosen for discussion. In fact, going on the assumption that there is a general interest amongst working-class communities in many of the articles serialised in the popular press, I ran a series of talks on subjects such as 'Naked Apes', 'Witchcraft', 'Life on the Planets', 'The Permissive Society'. The discussions took place in the public bar, not in a side room, for it was my intention to attract people to the discussions, hoping they would accept such an activity as they accept the TV or a musical group, something which they can take part in if they so wish.

In the event the series of discussions proved extremely successful. People were at first hesitant to join in, and some were only prepared to listen from a distance, but as the course continued more and more people took an active part. I acted as chairman, and I found it was necessary to interpret many of the things said by the speakers and also to reframe many of the questions for the audience. This illustrates some of Bernstein's findings about language codes and the problem of communication between cultural groups. The barrier is not so very difficult to cross, however, when a university professor can talk to EPA residents about evolution!

Although the emphasis was on enjoyment we did move purposely towards a discussion of local problems when a young minister gave a talk on the problems of American cities. It was relatively easy to draw parallels between the problems of cities in the US and the problems facing Liverpool. This gave rise to a great deal of debate on community involvement and many heard for the first time of the local community council and its work. Thus it was possible to move from a general interest situation to one of immediate concern without giving the impression that people were involved in the serious business of education.

In a house-to-house survey of one small section of the Liverpool EPA we found that some 20 per cent of those interviewed, mainly women, expressed an interest in such activities as hairdressing, keep fit, dressmaking. This is an area served by a local authority community centre offering these very activities! What were we to do? We decided to try to meet the demand in an informal manner. We booked a local church hall and invited all those who had expressed an interest to a meeting to organise the activities they wanted. In the event about half of those who expressed an interest turned up and we were able to set up 'classes' in hairdressing, keep fit and dressmaking, using volunteers from the local colleges of physical education and domestic science. There is no doubt that such activities provide a marvellous fillip to young mothers in areas of social and economic deprivation. We are also using these 'classes' to stimulate interest in other subjects by having a tutor-in-charge with responsibility for initiating discussions on topics of interest. This has proved very successful.

Because of the success of this type of work, i.e. in the pubs and in providing for the recreational interests of mothers, I have undertaken another survey in the Everton district of Liverpool with the assistance of diploma students from the Liverpool University Institute of Extension Studies. This exercise will be concerned with pinpointing all the social, recreational and religious groups which exist in the district. We then hope to discover how people's social and educational needs are being met and to what extent we can offer assistance either from our own resources or by using those of other educational organisations. This survey is being undertaken in close co-operation with the local community development officer, as the information we seek will be of great benefit to him in establishing links with and within the community and involving various community groups in some form of community action.

Adult Education as a Counselling Service

In the survey referred to above, although the general demand was for activities such as hairdressing and keep fit, nevertheless there were a number of scattered individuals who expressed interest in other subjects, such as languages, art, GCE courses, typewriting, psychology, and politics. This would seem to indicate that despite the publicity given to further education there are a number of people who are either unaware of the educational services available or lack the necessary know-how to take advantage of them. It can be argued that if people are determined they will take advantage of existing educational opportunities, but this view ignores the fact that for many people, in the sort of communities I have been dealing with, the whole business of joining a class in an institution is a totally new and frightening experience. Help is required, just as help is required when individuals have social problems, or problems to do with claiming welfare benefits.

Thus we intend to follow up the survey by offering individual advice and assistance to those who expressed interest in some form of further education outside the generally expressed interests for which we are already catering. In fact, during the past fourteen months, as I have got to know the people in the area, and my role has become clearer to them, I have already acted as counsellor to individuals seeking advice on GCE courses, WEA classes, extra-mural classes, entrance to Ruskin and other adult colleges.

As well as counselling individuals, I now find that as more and more people become aware of my work I am contacted by various community groups and professional workers in the field for advice and assistance on courses or classes they wish to run. In some instances, I can fill the need by using WEA resources, in others I can contact various educational agencies and ask for their assistance. My ability to undertake this service has proved of real benefit to a small band of committed professional and voluntary workers who have been nourishing little social groups for a number of years and undertaking a certain amount of informal adult education.[8] Because of their efforts adult education in the Liverpool EPA was not a completely barren field before I arrived on the scene.

Conclusion

The six roles of an adult education agency in an underprivileged community have been spelt out in some detail in order to emphasise the interrelated nature of the various roles and their total contribution to the process of community development. In other, more fortunate working-class communities it may not be necessary to adopt all the roles I have outlined and adult education may assume a more traditional format, but in an EPA (and similar communities both in the inner areas of our great cities and in some housing estates) it is essential that adult education should be closely integrated with other agencies and organisations – hence the concept of 'community adult education'.

In such a situation success cannot be reckoned solely in terms of the traditional 'class'. Certainly informal classes are possible, but most of the work that an adult education agency can undertake in an EPA cannot be brought within the scope of any set of educational regulations. As far as individuals are concerned success can be reckoned (though hardly measured) in terms of extension of vocabulary, increase in sociability, acquisition of communication skills, acceptance of the notion of cause and effect and of the notion of evidence, and other intangibles; but in the most important sense success will depend on the extent to which adult education contributes to the process of social change.

What has been done so far has been the promising work of a small group of individuals. It is much to be hoped that larger resources of personnel and finance can be devoted to this work.

References
1   T. Lovett, 'An experiment in Adult Education in the EPA', Occasional Paper No 8, Liverpool EPA Project.
2   'Helping yourself with your money', *Liverpool Daily Post*, 1 October 1970.
3   B. Bernstein, 'Social Class Language and Socialisation' (talk given to Liverpool Branch of the Association for Special Education on Thursday, 26 November 1970, in the Royal Institution, Liverpool).
4   T. Lovett, 'Holidays at Home', *Projectile* no 4, Autumn 1970 (Journal of the Liverpool EPA Project).
5   T. Shaw and T. Lovett, 'Adult Games – a revolutionary approach to Community Education', *Castle Street Circular*, November 1970 (Liverpool Council of Social Service).

6   Schools Council/Nuffield Humanities Project, *The Humanities Project: an Introduction* (1970).

7   National Marriage Guidance Council, *Annual Report, 1969–70.*

8   J. Saxby, 'Helping Young Mothers to Cope', *National Council for Social Service Quarterly*, Autumn 1968.

5

Education at the Bottom

DAVID HEAD
(Studies in Adult Education, 9, 1977.)

I. Intentions

Territory

Education is invasion. The more usual word is 'intervention', pin-pointing the external origin of the operation. 'Invasion' suggests a 'hostile inroad'[1] with its overtones of occupation, cultural imposition, and invading strategy. We may like to think of education, paradoxically, as a 'friendly invasion'; but it may happen that the educator is seen not as a friendly power to be welcomed, but as an alien power to be repulsed. Either way, the territory of the learner is occupied by change-bringing forces.

In adult education we respond to demand. In practice, this usually means flying a kite to see who runs after it. But even if the demand comes unsought (which is unusual) and we see our business as simply to meet it (which few of us do), we respond by the introduction of educators, inevitably with their own ideas of what is 'worthwhile'.[2] When classes are set up on other people's premises, the invasion is physical as well as cultural. The territory of a community centre, or a home for the elderly, becomes occupied by persons, equipment and activities none of which may have been asked for. The intention is to draw into 'worthwhile' activities people to whom it would never occur to go to an adult education centre, or who could not or would not do so. Of course, they do not have to join in.

When these classes take place on premises catering for dependent people, they are usually referred to as 'welfare classes'. It is a give-away phrase, conjuring up ideas (to delight or repel us, according to our social philosophy) of providing a bonus activity for the deprived. What difference would it make to exchange a wel*fare* concept for a concept of 'well-being' – including 'being for oneself'? Those demanding *educational* justification for such classes – educational theory and public money being at stake – may find it in that same idea of 'well-being'.

What kind of learning attends this particular type of educational invasion? This article looks at one such project.

We have all seen people walking the pavements aimlessly, with bundles and sometimes bottles, some remote and alone, some stopping to search litter bins or waylay a passer-by; and we are oblivious or repulsed or conscience-stricken or momentarily disturbed – but life, and we (and they?), must go on. The Kingsway Day Centre, Holborn, London WC2 was set up four years ago with such people in mind. It is the only day-care facility available to older single homeless men in the West End; used also by a handful of women, and a few young people (for whom other centres exist). Users vary considerably, and have their own social distinctions.[3] They include hard-drinking ex-naval men, many people from broken families, some physically disabled or mentally handicapped, quiet shadows of men over retirement age, short- and long-term unemployed, the 'unemployable', some with prison records, and some who have rejected the 'normal' patterns of work, routine, and respectability. Some sleep rough, others are reluctant users of hostels, a few squat precariously.

The staff see 'The Kingsway' as primarily for people socially at rock bottom,

> *. . . offering shelter free from social tensions which clients suffer in society, and minimal aids for the maintenance of physical standards*[4]

Aids include the services of visiting nurse and barber, endlessly flowing sweet tea, soup at midday, razors and shoe-cleaning materials, needles and thread, water and soap, and the use of the telephone for 'business' calls. The centre is open on weekdays only, from 10.30 to 3.30, with a full-time staff of four and three regular volunteers. The maximum number admitted at any one time is a hundred; most sit around in silence, a few talk with animation, some play games. Staff help with information, and refer people to other agencies concerned with accommodation, alcoholism, etc:

> *The philosophy is based on personal contact between workers and clients. The establishment of caring relationships can help the clients' lives become more bearable, and can lead to greater awareness of the possibilities open to them.*

That last phrase might have led the centre's organisers to consider some forms of educational activity; but largely because of limited staff and resources, nothing was ever laid on, except a small cupboard of books to be borrowed, and the chance to play chess, snooker, or a far-from-grand piano.

Bridgehead
In late 1975 invasion came from the City Lit – a centre for adult studies

with a 'literary institute' history, and geographically near. My appointment as tutor in community education in the Adult Education Training Unit included the exploration of neighbourhood-based education in line with the City Lit programme and resources; with the blessing of the local Adult Education Institute. An adult literacy project was established, its particular style arising from its central-city location and the influence of the socio-linguistic approach pioneered by Paulo Freire. The question was raised with staff at The Kingsway whether this activity could be usefully extended to the centre. We decided to see if a group could be set up of people interested in reading, writing and discussing – rather than literacy; and rather than crafts, which might smack of 'occupational therapy'.

There was help from a student on placement from a course on social work. We tried to come to terms with the risks of 'invasion' techniques, and the likelihood of taking responsibility away from people at the moment when we were trying to do the opposite; as educator and social worker we could reflect bifocally. The bridgehead was a regular hour's visit a week, just being around, with the possibility of a group meeting at 3.30 when the centre closed. It was hard going. Very few of the centre's users had any idea why we were there, and we wondered ourselves. A few were happy to talk. Most cared so little about our presence as not even to be suspicious.

The first response to personal invitations to stay behind came from a middle-aged man recently become 'dry', who was interested in applying for a job with alcoholics, but found writing letters and reports hard going. The following week another man stayed behind, wanting to write to a friend in prison. The week after, neither appeared, but two others (one much the worse for wear) stayed for a chat. Advance came with the use of notices. One behind the tea counter, put up by a member of staff with his own brand of humour, invited anyone interested in reading and writing to stay. He spelt it 'wrighting' – and soon a slip of paper underneath, written in uneven capitals, swore at the 'ignorant bastards' running the place. Our first piece of creative writing! What happened next is best indicated by a diary extract:

> *In the first hour we met M, a quiet extrovert who showed us a prayer he had written in 'Old English' script. It asked the Lord to keep his mouth shut until he had something to say. (M is always afraid of speaking out of turn.) He says he'll stay afterwards. W is tall, early 20s. I'm introduced to him while he's playing snooker; when he's finished, he stands in the middle of the room reading to me from his loose-leaf file of poems. He'll stay if his girl-friend does; she won't but says he can; he decides not to. H, who has been knowledgeable about London history, also goes; he's afraid somebody will think he has stayed for help with reading.*

At 3.30 'Mad R', *broad, big-bearded, taciturn, hangs around. K puts the lights out; his way of showing disapproval of after-meetings, since his job is to tidy up. He goes off to sweep the other room, so we put them on again. C has joined us, with sharp Scottish accent, and razor-edged comment. So has J who, not being able to bring bottles into the centre, has drunk it all first; he sleeps noisily throughout. A deaconess from the Mission upstairs looks in, and stays.*

We begin by trying to explain why we are there, and why we want to start a group; not easy, as we are not at all clear ourselves. We talk a little about the uses of reading, and the problems that can arise for people only partly literate. We want to see if talking, writing, reading and other group pursuits can be of use to people in the centre.

M, with agonising diffidence laced with pride, announces that he has just started to write his life story, and has filled the first 5 pages of his fat old diary. Will he read to us? 'No fear, I'm going pink already.' So others read for him:

THE PRIVATE LIFE OF M. G. J. FROM WOMB TO TOMB: CHIEF CONTESTANT FOR NOBEL PEACE PRIZE LITERARY AWARD

I was born on a cold wintry day in November. I first saw the light of day in a maternity hospital. I was difficult at birth, difficult as a child, and frankly I've been difficult ever since . . .

It is full of vivid memories of boyhood games, the antagonism of his father, and his intense love for his mother, who died. We are all attending, C with scorn, Mad R inscrutable, M himself utterly still. Only J is unmoved, in oblivion. Half-way through the reading, we are told that the hotel next door is on fire, but there is an exit if we need it. At the end, it is hard to assure M that we liked it, until Mad R suddenly stirs himself. 'It's just like Dickens,' he says.

As we chat about it, P arrives, his skin and hair show an Asian origin, as do his words which go on and on. 'I want to learn to speak', he shouts, but he already speaks in an unstoppable rush of bubbling metaphors. It is all about birth and death and reincarnation, and breeze and Britain, and fire and god. Babble. Poetry. 'They all say I'm mad,' he says as he goes. 4.30 and we go. Since first coming, I've already spent 24 hours on the premises. What about tangible results? What hope of development?

After this small but heady tot of success, we discuss with staff how we might interest others, and decide to invite the men to come to the City Lit to make a video programme, which could be brought to the centre to show the rest what was going on.

The invitation, somewhat to our surprise, was taken up. After lively preliminary discussions, fourteen people (including some members of staff) produced
a tape which included readings and discussions – one man drawing his
nightmare in charcoal and discussing the significance of the tiny lame figure
in the long corridor – comic impressions, interviews and questions to staff
about their motives. It was later shown to seventy people in the day centre.

Objectives

Since then the group has fluctuated widely with sometimes two, often seven
or eight, up to a mass-meeting of about twenty-five. For many months there
was little continuity; now some people make a point of being at the centre on
Thursdays. Activities have included play-readings, writing on a theme, games
with words, poetry readings, sharing information about events (e.g. places to
go over Christmas), discussion about how to improve conditions – including
those at the centre itself, planning a magazine, drawing and crayoning, writing
letters and reading replies (when they come), arguing about facts, and all the
time sharing experiences, voicing antagonisms, and expressing support.

What does it mean to the people who stay? The purpose of on-site classes
is to make it as easy as possible for people to attend. For the student, a
minimum of motivation is required. Indeed, it is hardly appropriate to use
the word 'student', since it is unlikely that anyone stays with a particular
learning intention – unless it be to 'learn' what is going on! It would be
facile to make a sharp contrast between this outer limit or purposelessness
and the assumed intentions of students attending adult education centres.
True, some of these have a clear idea of what they come for (basic skills of
motor-cycle maintenance, the implications of the latest Housing Act) and may
not be seen again; but many come looking for a congenial social experience
allied to a practical or intellectual interest. The Kingsway group may not be
so out-of-the-way as it appears.

Going on what members of the group say, their motives include curiosity,
something to do, a liking for others around, the chance of an audience, some
idea that this is a serious activity that will enhance status (if only in their
own eyes), or the desire of people 'out' of almost everything to be 'in' on
something.

An even more powerful motive might be the chance of an extra hour warm
and dry. That being so, the fact that often so few people stay would seem
to indicate (in addition to ignorance of what is going on) a widely shared
reluctance to get involved. We can only speculate on the reasons: It's not
for people like us, or it's not interesting, or it's the usual crowd who like
the sound of their own voices, or we don't take to visitors who think they
know what's good for us, or we might expose our ignorance, or it looks like

some sort of regimentation, or there are people there we don't like. As with adult education in general, it is much more difficult to discover why people *don't* take advantage of what we provide, and why they are not attracted by what we think we have made attractive.

If those who are attracted, however ambiguously, do not come to learn – let alone to learn some specific thing, let alone be taught – then any educational objectives are initially the tutor's. Initial ignorance of the 'single homeless' scene has one great advantage: you do not set your sights low to correspond to some preconception of what is or is not feasible. And the casual conversations about farming, travel, art exhibitions, work, relationships – as well as seamier subjects – never let you forget that 'we also have brains'.

The ideology behind the outreach activities that characterise much 'community education' sees the aim as identifying people's needs. The adjective 'educational' is implicit, and the operation resembles that of community workers who invade a territory with the purpose (whether of the institution they work for, or their own) of changing situations and attitudes. The word 'need' implies that *we* have set some standards for human living, or for a democratic and educated society, which people do not come up to.[5]

Working at The Kingsway, we had to come to terms with this. We believed it is better to be housed and fed than homeless and hungry; and few there would have regarded such ideas as an invasion. We also believed that over-dependence and one-sided dependence are dehumanising; that to be human is to have access to cultural riches, to have choices and some say in your circumstances, to have a voice in making changes for the better, to be entitled to dignity and to the sense of being of value to others; perhaps many there would agree with that too, if only as a lost dream. But how many other class- and culture-conditioned values did we bring with us, and what hidden objectives arising from our own unidentified motives? Concern about such invasions arises in two ways. First, these are people who constantly find themselves at the receiving end of other people's hand-outs. Is education to be one more hand-out, no less dehumanising than the rest? Secondly, if people think they are being 'got at', they will not be inclined to respond in a positive way. At The Kingsway, the invasion is particularly hard to cover up, since all the available facilities – from chairs to shoe polish, from shelter to snooker – are meeting an obvious need. Then who are these people imposed on us? What are their motives? Coming from that world which despises us, and blames us because we make problems for them, what do they want to do to us? To improve us!

As an educator, you may want to express the situation very differently. But it may also dawn on you that you *are* trying to improve them in the name of education, or why are you there at all? At the same time, your courage to be there may be based on the faith that the model of 'solidarity' can sometimes, some way, supersede the deeply-ingrained model of 'service'.[6] You want to be with them, 'on their side', never to put them in the position of objects.

How can this happen? First, by trying – in the face of puzzlement and suspicion – to clarify to yourself *and to them* what sort of improvement you intend. At least the concept of improvement (however unacceptable in most forms) far transcends any 'welfare' idea of making people happy or less bored; both worthy aims, but education has a stronger purpose.

Secondly, you can correct your own education-prompted attempts to think up 'worthwhile' activities, by finding out what is worthwhile *to them* which calls for an educational response, thus taking the centre users with total seriousness. They have expressed no wish to learn anything, but what at an adult education centre would be a 'subject' interest has its equivalent in people who stay ('stay' not 'come') having some idea of what they are in for. There may have been gossip about the group's activities. Negatively, they know they are *not* staying for games, crafts, group therapy, moral instruction, party politics, or religious exercises. They also know it is a *group* activity. (Doubtless that keeps some away.) Further, they may see it linking up with what could be of practical use to them, or with their current interests – with the added satisfaction of having someone to listen.

On these inklings, rather than on any prior educational ideas (though these will doubtless intrude) can be built an approach, a method, and a choice of activities.

II. Extensions

Extension of interest

The approach could hardly be simpler: to extend what is of interest and of use. Comparisons can be drawn with adult educational ideas that mingle in the concept of 'extending the subject' – that is, identifying the broader and deeper implications, so that flower arrangement can take up ecological issues and cookery can include a look into the wages of sugar-plantation workers. Extension in day-centre terms is of continuing and spontaneous interests, of part-hidden talents and latent ideas, by widening their range, increasing and finding outlets for skills, analysing social dimensions, or reflecting with others on the significance of events.

This is no matter of beginning where people are to take them where we think it would be good for them to go; though educational method often seems to follow that path. Certainly, we cannot avoid having our own ideas about worthy destinations, but if we are to avoid the worst aspects of invasion, our aim must be to begin where people are and discover with them *where it is worth going*. In practice, there seems to be some common agreement at The Kingsway that there is value in an extension of communication and expression, of self-confidence and self-respect, of other-help to self-help to mutual help.

Some of the most creative aspects of day-centre life include relationships, the practical things people do for each other – tea-making, decorating, cleaning up, etc., some of which carry an allowance – the social art of conversation, and the more private activities of drawing and reading. Some read insatiably, so the library cupboard can become a meeting place, and the group can discuss books and have playreadings. Drawing, too, is very popular with some. It can be encouraged by supplies of paper, pens, and colours; and extended by using the visual images as the start of putting feelings into words. The latest plan is to get people painting murals. Like everything else in the rock-bottom struggle to survive, drawing takes on distinctive meaning:

> *Like sex, I like drawing spontaneous like. You do understand, don't you? To tell the truth, I only draw at the centre when I want to see if my hand's steadied up after my head's been bad. Out of doors, it's different, It's the law, you see. They're always moving me on – keep asking me what I'm up to. If I draw a building or something, they leave me be.*

Art work is a means of release and self-expression. After all, a root cause of many of the users' problems is in human relationships that have radically not functioned for them; and art can be shared, and discussed.

Talk can be bitter, but it still represents human contact. M wrote,

> *It's good when you can talk to people about everyday happenings and current affairs, and a congenial attitude develops arising out of common sense and practical mindedness.*

Why not make a special extension on Thursdays? M's comment came out of one of the occasions when an agenda was proposed. To promote the sharing of experiences, it was agreed that people would write something round the two ideas, I LIKE IT WHEN . . . and I HATE IT WHEN . . . The results, which were read out and discussed, underlined our kinship in the things we value. For instance, our feelings depend a lot on other people's attitudes; we hate being judged by first impressions, and a day can be ruined by 'verbal violence'. The moods of nature affect our moods. We want security, and the chance to be of use to people 'to make them sure of themselves in such a very unreal and unsure environment'. We like to live our own life, however unsatisfactory it is to us, and we hate it when other people keep telling us what to do. It's a special joy 'when I can go to my own room at night'. There was also a comment about the group:

> *I like it when Thursday comes around for getting down to the centre and letting my hair down.*

It would be an interesting exercise to try to rewrite that statement in educational terms!

Writing, then, can be an extension of feeling and thought. It is also at times a necessary chore (letters, forms), and can be a lifeline. H is disabled and cannot work. When asked privately why he stayed on Thursdays, his answer was, 'Because of that tripe, that eye-wash.' That is how he describes (and dismisses) his writing 'if you can call it writing'. His stories have been typed up, and he maintains an indestructible optimism about them. When he thinks of all the doss-houses he would like to avoid for the rest of his life

> *... the only thing that's going to stop me is that story when it gets into print ... I've got a good idea what this writing will open up for me, I don't care what anybody says.*

But, of course, he does care, and his bravado easily turns to gloom: 'When you write something, who's going to look at it?' So why does he write? Because it does him a lot of good, and keeps him from going nuts.

W, too, talks about the satisfaction he gets in expressing himself on paper. He likes to read some of his ninety-six poems to others, to help him get deeper into people. Contact is essential: 'I get a lot of experience from other people. I put myself in their position.' In his poetry the vagueness of his own goals in life finds expression in the experience of being 'On the Road':

> *Where I'm going no-one will know,*
> *It's how far I walk or how far I stroll.*

An outlet for these and other more casual writers has been an issue of a magazine, named the *Kingsway Herald*[7], a duplicated production of twenty pages, containing poems, articles, reminiscences, puzzles, drawings, stories, letters and comments. Twenty-two people signed on as the editorial committee, though few seemed to think it would ever happen. It was decided that the magazine should not only be distributed free in the centre, but sold at the City Lit so that people could 'find out how people in the Day Centre live'. The tone was set in a poem about the centre, describing the dossers, most of whom 'have given up, flotsam in the tideway of the world'. After describing the plastic cups, the soup, and the anger, the poem ends,

> *But me, the monotony of the radio*
> *Is all that's left to me –*
> *Love doesn't rule this world, selfishness*
> *Is just a pretty notion destroyed*
> *At birth by lack of succour.*
> *Yet I see gladness in some eyes,*
> *Here in this dossers' refuge.*

In such ways, then, one thing leads to another. For a few, the extension of their interest spills out beyond The Kingsway. Some of the younger people have got involved with craft activities at another local centre; others have linked up with the local adult literacy project. A few have begun to use the City Lit itself. Some have come to put interviews on video, and to learn how to use the equipment. F has joined an art class, and E a music group. And G, with exceptional artistic gifts, has often said he will join a class, but always turns back with, 'What's the use?'

This is the question which has led people in the group to ask what might be *done*, with a wavering confidence that chat, writing, or anything else can make the slightest difference to their existence. *Is* there an extension into action?

Extension into action
Words easily become false currency unless they have a use. It is a dilemma of 'community education' that, while individuals can go away and put words into practice, group action leading to change (as distinct from speech and thought leading to change) is too involved, too ambiguous, too controversial to be part of a statutory educational programme. This is unfortunate, since so much learning is by doing, and learning about society by social doing.

Could talk in the group about undernourishment, low casual wages, or homelessness lead anywhere? What *use* was it? For four weeks running, the group discussed the problems of being 'of no fixed abode', the uncertainties of squats, and the stigma that clings to hostel-livers. Contact was made with CHAR (Campaign for Single Homeless People)[8] to find out what programme was being promoted, and how the group's findings could be of use to its continuing work. Out of the discussions, a letter was prepared.

It began by making scathing and wholly justified remarks about the conditions in a local hostel housing several hundred men, and went on to point out that most of the problems of hostels are caused because they *are* hostels:

> *Why do we have to live in hostels year-in, year-out, with our social security benefits geared to hostel rates? These hostels were intended for emergencies, but are full of regulars who book in week after week . . .*
>
> *What we need is decent accommodation suitable for single persons to live in with some independence and self-respect. Some of the day-centre people have recently become tenants in a short-life house. The property has not been turned into a slum, nor wrecked, nor burnt down. But because of our present circumstances, people do not want us as neighbours, and do not want to give us lodgings.*

The letter went on to underline the lack of bed-sitting rooms, and of council policy, and it asked for some action. It was sent to the appropriate bodies, signed THURSDAYS AT 3.30.

No replies were ever received. The manager of the offending hostel phoned the staff to find out what was going on; he said he would treat the letter as he treated all anonymous letters. But a local councillor saw it, and took up the hostel complaints.

There are still repercussions. The letter was quoted in full in the CHAR news-sheet, and by a group looking for more property for single homeless people. It also brought to the Thursday meetings a small group of ex-dossers and helpers working for PROD (Preservation of the Rights of Dossers) to see if they could recruit support for their organisation; in the event, few wanted to get involved. And the letter has led to continuing correspondence; so the group does not feel it was quite useless. Since then the group has worked on a further document dealing with the experiences and entitlements of people of 'no fixed address'.

'Useful' activity is not, however, confined to work towards social or political change, though indeed very little will change for the better without it. Activities are useful if they give a chance to display skill – in talking or in giving information or (as on one occasion) in playing the spoons; or if they touch (however obliquely) upon some issue needing a certain distancing; or if (however unintended) they lead to self-discovery and insights into debilitating circumstances; or if they lead to that strange blending of engagement and escape that goes with artistic productions; or if they help to turn troubles into problems to be tackled; or if they give you enough courage to limit your fantasising.

But surely people have to find their own opportunities for such things, and make use of them: what is the use of an organised group with a tutor-invader? For some the question is not even worth asking. One of the more self-respecting users of the centre sat watching the group in action, with a handful of people present including the noisy and disruptive. Looking towards the tutor, he whispered to a neighbour, 'Do they *pay* him to come here? They must be mad.' If group activity has any use (and it certainly has some users) it must be as an extension of what is already being found interesting and of value. In what ways?

Extension through group work
A possible starting-point is an incident lasting only a few seconds:

> *About ten of us were discussing the proposed magazine, and reading two contributions that had been brought. In the group were F, a girl in her twenties, and the man she goes around with. They were openly distracted. They'd been arguing before they sat down, and they brought the atmosphere with them. The dispute broke out again. It was about where she would spend the night. He wasn't well, and was booked in at a men's hostel. She said if she couldn't be with him, she'd sleep rough. Others joined in and made suggestions, which were all resisted. Suddenly D rose to his feet, stretching out his arm and pointing at her with a trembling hand:*
> *'Don't be a ... fool. I'm a ... fool, and that's why I'm epileptic. Don't be a fool like me. Go to a hostel. Do you want to be raped in the streets?'*

Shaken by the onslaught and by the heated concern, she said she might go. On reflection, this raises a number of issues about the group:

1. Because the atmosphere was a free-for-all, occasionally pushed along with a minimum of fuss, nobody felt that the group was being spoilt or the tutor slighted. Those present because of their interest in the magazine were far more interested in the personal and the immediate. In an educational class following a curriculum, the 'hidden agendas' have to be handled, diverted, or repressed, so that the group can 'get on with the job'. This group was never without some 'job', but perhaps its main agenda *was* the hidden agenda of its members.

2. The particular 'content' of a night's lodging was a vital matter for all the members. Their experience was wide and bitter, and the problems were recurring. Such resource as there was came not from us (our accommodation problems were of a different order) but from others in the group with the expertise. So there were no problems of participation.

3. Nor was the group coincidental to the outburst. D seldom says a word in the group; it takes a lot to rouse him. The dramatic style suggested that

this was not just two people arguing. He was aware of the group and the tutor; he was taking the stage; he was doing what we all find the need to do – explaining himself publicly. Because of his own disabilities and frustrations, he has moments of irrational violence. In this instance, his aggressiveness was channelled into concern for another person, expressed with an untypical authority.

4. His action showed heightened feeling, but with 'common sense' reasoning which opened up new possibilities of rational discussion. This was no exercise in group therapy, but it was therapeutic none the less. F's insistence on taking to the streets was recognised as a way of reacting to 'them', who by their arrangements were keeping her and her man apart. When you are down, so much of what you do is a futile self-destructive kicking on doors, as the only way of expressing disgust. Perhaps the chance of opening her misery to others, and to argument, helped her to change her mind.

5. It is not uncommon for one or two people to dominate the group for a period. Many who come are individualists to a high degree; once they want to say something, they no longer hear the person talking at the time. (We all know classes like that.) The group frequently breaks into smaller units. We usually prefer not to try to call them together, telling ourselves that the exercise has changed to 'buzz' groups! On other occasions, members themselves have taken responsibility for keeping the group together, as when one wanderer to the snooker table was quietly brought back.

6. D's self-depreciation was in sharp contrast with the power of his intervention. He has never worked; he said once that he'd been pushed from pillar to post all through his life. He has often been as negative about the group as he is about himself. Communication? 'You might as well speak to the brick wall, and you'll get an answer.' Now here he was, speaking to that brick wall. Perhaps the Thursday group can promote such 'richness of individual response'.[9]

We now add a No 7 to those reflections: In that incident, there was no role for the tutor! But without the 'invasion' there would have been no group. Much has been written about experimental roles adopted by educators, replacing 'teacher' by 'enabler', 'facilitator', *'animateur'*, or whatever. All would seem to demand an openness to change, and a contribution as both outsider and friend. Except in institutional contexts or professional relationships, users of The Kingsway get little chance to tangle with members of the 'outside' world. Such contact has a lot of significance, whether what they long for is to be more accepted or to 'pick bones'. The value of the encounter loses much if the tutor comes across as just one more professional who 'knows better than I do what is good for me'.

A friend then? Community and educational workers know only too well in their work the conflicting necessities of being involved and keeping some distance. To be called, as on one occasion, 'one of the boys, sort of' is a kind of compliment, but the 'sort of' cries loudly of the vast social differences that overshadow the human similarities. Yet the model of friendship cannot be bettered, in so far as a friend is one who takes me and my interests seriously, who helps me to identify what is important to me, who shows me new vistas and invites me to explore them, who makes possible a relationship where we mutually contribute to each other or (we might say) invade each other's territory of perceptions, values and intentions.

At The Kingsway, we are out to extend not only interests and activities, but the learner too, and also ourselves.[10] There are many parallels with the role of so-called 'extension workers' in countries much concerned with development. The presence of such workers in rural areas has its objective, not only in the increase of agricultural production and economic growth, but also in extending the sights and insights of local leaders. But such extension work, whether in field, factory, classroom, or day centre, is open to all the dangers of 'cultural imperialism' which Freire exposes so sharply.[11]

III. Tensions

Education and excellence

This may be invasion, but is it education? The Thursday group has no 'subject', no syllabus, little that is systematic, no teaching in the usual sense. It provides no training that opens vocational doors, and produces no measurable change in those who come.

These are the criteria often put forward as educational. Among those at The Kingsway, however, the concept of education is richer and more elusive. They will say that education is what they were taught at school – 'history, names in history, geography and the like' – and some will list their achievements. Others will share memories of failure, and for their sake the word 'education' is better avoided on Thursdays, if something of what it stands for is to happen.[12] The educated person, they say, is one who 'talks in an educated way', the sort of person who retains knowledge – as one man said, 'It goes in one ear-hole and does not come out of the other' – the sort of person who can operate equipment, and can improve his skills. He is someone who learns by experience and can change his line of action as a result. For H this relates to the kind of 'doss-houses' available:

> *You go in there once, and you don't want to go in there again. That is what is called learning.*

These educational hunches are as interesting for what they stress as for what they underplay.

Education has to do with the transmission of culture ('talk', 'knowledge'). To be human is to inherit a particular culture through custom, literature, history, not forgetting the underlying economic and political structures; and through all the experiences of growing up and extending adult experience within a particular society. This is to see education as

> . . . *initiation into activities, modes of conduct and thought, which have standards written into them.*[13]

The standards relate to what is publicly acknowledged to be the best of the culture. This raises a number of problems. One has to do with that word 'publicly', which must refer to dominant values in the society. Another concerns the monopoly which education has come to hold over social initiation.[14] Another is the passivity of the learner which is implicit in that statement. In what H said about the doss-houses, there is the hint of the need for a creative, critical response to what is being transmitted.

This dialectical movement between culture and person, which is the continual pattern of human experience, is also reflected in assertions that education is about the actualising of human possibilities. At The Kingsway we are told that education is about personal skills and knowhow, but these things are seen in very individualistic terms. There is no hint that what you do has some effect on the world around you. This recognition was basic to Freire's consciousness-raising programme, which affirmed that to be human is to '*make*' history. In his approach, water supplies, and hat trimmings, and political revolution, are all expressions of the human vocation of re-making culture. While not throwing the net quite so wide, adult education in the United Kingdom has traditionally seen its goal as 'the good life of the civilised man in a civilised society'.[15]

It follows that, in the pursuit of 'excellence', education both puts me in touch with the world which my fellow human beings have made, and invites me to respond personally to it and to work with others to reshape it. Is this a useful approach for educators drinking sweet tea at The Kingsway? Questions form on the lips as the mug leaves them: If education is 'initiation into a tradition', what is there in it for a socially-labelled or self-confessed 'deviant'? And what potential has a person despairingly occupied with existing at survival level?

And further: what happens when 'what is out there' has become cold, alien and threatening? Education, as the reflection of society, becomes very much of an invasion, a 'hostile inroad'. And what happens when 'what is in me' is a further alienation, compounded of fantasy, impotence, and self-disgust? Education, with its aim in self-fulfilment, sounds like mockery.

Culture and sub-culture

Public stigmatisation of frequenters of The Kingsway has a wide sweep, tarring them all with the same brush: their appearance is offensive; they dodge work and live off hand-outs; they have no fixed abode (this is the official label of people who have lived in the same hostel for years); they are alcoholics, drug-addicts, criminals; they are neither savers nor consumers.

Part true, part false, like other generalisations conceived in hostility. In reality, their relationship with 'what is out there' – a social culture with its educationally transmitted values – is complex. For many, the 'rot' set in with a breakdown in health, mental stability, family relationships, or morale. They found themselves victims of circumstances, beyond the limits of coping, drained of self-respect. As poverty bites, doors slam. Many experiences were distilled into one statement in the group's letter:

> *What you have done is to turn us into hostel dwellers, and forced us to adopt a way of life you disapprove of.*

When you have battered in vain on the door into the 'acceptable' world, you reach the conclusion that it is barred on the inside: 'they' are making it impossible for you. As a result, you become subdued, fatalistic, dependent on benevolent scraps. Or you kick out against those who represent authority.[16] Or you go independent, live by casual labour, and reject those 'publicly shared norms and values' said to be the basis of education.

What this adds up to is a variety of attitudes and stances within one identifiable subculture – one because of the use of the same institutions, similar hassles, shared survival problems, and the same tightly-drawn options (as between the indignity of a resettlement centre and the consequences of sleeping rough). You have entered this subculture, not as a revolutionary alternative, but because there was nowhere else to go.

Arrangements made by local authorities and government departments make it appear, again and again, that society is excluding such people because of their way of life, and at the same time blaming and punishing them for being excluded.[17] As one result, they miss out on cultural opportunities most of us take for granted. For one thing, they can't afford them – except the occasional film or bet, or books from second-hand shops or bins. For another, there is nowhere to keep personal belongings safe. But, chiefly, public places like museums, libraries, and recreational centres insist that they move on. Nor can we be confident that well-supported centres of adult education will not be indignant and icy-cold if this sort of person comes in – in spite of all the current concern for the 'disadvantaged'; indeed, is it entirely cynical to trace here a less worthy reason for on-site courses?

Thus one educational justification of the Thursday group is the access it gives to people otherwise denied access. It may remind them that, in spite of all ostracisation, they are inheritors of a culture; and hence part of the human species. In spite of enforced cultural poverty, they can enjoy the insights of poets and playwrights, discuss their experiences of other places and times, swop jokes and paperbacks, express judgements on music and art, read the Bible with identification, and sharpen their critical wits. Can those without belongings have a sense of belonging, and the rootless feel their roots?

Then what of those rooted in the culture, but alienated from the society? Is it part of the educator's task to try to 'rehabilitate the outsider'? The answer must be 'No', but the question is nothing like so simple as it looks.

The social workers themselves are pulled in different directions. They may want by every means to get people out of the cold and discomfort, alcoholism and petty crime, self-despising and despair.[18] That may not be quite the same thing as trying to restore them to a 'socially acceptable routine'.[19] True, many long to be accepted. Then do the modest comforts of the day centre make this more difficult, as one user put it, 'by encouraging us to be lazy'?

But workers also know that some will live on the streets till they die. So they want to help them make something of a bad job. At best, this brings support to those who have chosen to live rough, as the best of a rotten bunch of choices (like living with people you can't live with, or with regulations and restrictions you won't live with). At worst, it works on the assumption that there *is* no way either back or forward, so all that is left is to establish an identity as a social outcast.[20]

Sharing these tensions, I cannot, as the tutor, do much anyway. Educational invasion has the object neither of improving facilities, nor lobbying politically – though it may lead me into some private-life commitments. Neither am I paid to produce, any more than to subvert, conformists. Those who see education in strongly ethical terms may want to thrust the role of rehabilitator upon me. But for the sake of the people and professional integrity, I must resist them.

I am not there to manipulate people, even after the most 'acceptable' social models, or even according to the most humane insights. But neither am I there simply to wait to be used (like an invader awaiting capture), nor without my own points of view. All my work is in dialogue, within which I have to attend unreservedly (but not uncritically) to what matters to the others. And it will be educational to the extent that it invites an exploration into what is 'human'.

It does this not by producing tailor-made people, but by supplying thread and patterns; not by entering a fixed tradition, but by working on that tradition; not only by grasping what others meant, but by finding personal meanings. For users of The Kingsway, the Thursday group may help them to know where they are and why, and to find ways more acceptable to *them* of being there or of moving on. It may also remind them that where they are is not the whole universe. And where the cry is for some inner satisfaction that may strengthen the hands to shape outward conditions, education is a resource.

Potential and self-definition

Education is a resource; but what if the hand is too preoccupied or too weak to grasp it?

As we unravel that strand of educational legitimacy sometimes expressed as 'fulfilling potential', we may sense its incongruity with the circumstances of those lacking basic shelter, food, sexual satisfaction and social life; who do without such advertised accoutrements of individuality as possessions, financial independence, family security, livelihood and leisure; who affirm no congenial social alternatives.

Education is supposed to help us 'to live wisely and agreeably and well', but it cannot help towards goals like achieving under the stars a warm, undisturbed night's lodging; dossers know more about that than professors. It is a common social attitude to make demands on people, while denying the fundamental problems which confront them. Hence the comment of one of the dispossessed, who finds jobs and independence eluding him: 'The people are the social problem, not the wino's'. There are severe limits to what can be done by educators, or any other invaders, so long as society 'does not want to know' or makes the victim the problem. To what extent do we tutors also deny the problem, by organising educational activity among those whose needs are immediate and down-to-earth? If we were really concerned about 'potential', should we not put our energies into housing – as Mr Peabody did in London in the last century, believing that people could then find their own happiness in life. (One of his estates is just up the road from The Kingsway.) But our gifts and employment lie elsewhere! Very well, but we must then realise that others may be making a more effective contribution to our educational goals than we are.

What can education achieve within existing circumstances? It might awaken or re-awaken elements of personality which are dormant or repressed – but that might only increase the agony if the basic problems remain untackled. It might help to develop practical skills, and to find ways out of the ditch, but it is up against a formidable obstacle: namely, that educational work designed to *fulfil* is being attempted in an atmosphere that *suppresses*.

The subculture we spoke of is a subculture of impotence. It may often be true that nothing can be done, but behind that is the conviction that 'our sort can do nothing'. There is neither the opportunity, nor the will. Previous experiences of failure in relationships, in attempts to stay sober, in struggles to escape the dog-house, in careers of petty crime, conspire with present debilitating circumstances to destroy the muscle to act. There is no doubting the possibilities: at The Kingsway there is not only silent withdrawal, but comradeship and insight and humour to be envied; but these are the linings of a subculture characterised by defeat. As has been said of families on low income in bad housing, energy is locked up in the battle for survival in an alien social world.[21] That being so, *any* educational tapping of potential will depend on the day-centre's own undemanding, congenial character as 'a shelter free from social tensions'.

But if problems cannot be solved externally, and the sense of powerlessness prevents people from dealing with their own problems, might we not just as well all go home (those of us who have homes to go to)? No, there is more. Behind the practical problems is the deeper problem of self-definition. A prior question is how people come to see themselves through different eyes, and become more open-eyed about their circumstances. The things that go on at The Kingsway show people, socially at rock bottom, to be still concerned with self-esteem and with projecting a better image of themselves.

Clearly, our self-appraisal is affected by our social contacts, and how others see us. The effect may be dismally negative, which is why hell is other people. But to be affirmed by others is an essential step to self-affirmation.

We also need to feel we are useful; which is extremely hard for those self-consciously dependent on hand-outs. Community workers, confronting the subculture of impotence, bring evidence that involvement in some form of social action redefines the poor and the powerless. But that itself can be overbearing. We have noted the resistance to joining pressure groups. More recently, the Thursday group has been in tentative touch with local community work schemes which could employ some of the more skilled as well as labourers. Such schemes could change local attitudes to the workers, as well as the workers' own self-image. But in the subculture of impotence, such projects are a long haul.

The final question is whether the impotent people can redefine themselves through *educational* activity? Such activity may itself suppress potential, if the group becomes yet another experience of being at the receiving end of the providers of the 'good'. This may also apply to other welfare classes, where handicapped people may be made, if not 'professional victims' then 'professional students', always the helped and taught, rather than autonomous and responsible learners. It need not be so, however. Given the right climate, energy can be unlocked to fulfil social and personal ends. This depends on many factors: on the style of the educational invasion, and how far it recognises entitlement to dignity; on the attitude of tutors and how much genuine faith they have in others; on the success of modest examples of problem-solving, like producing a magazine or pursuing a craft-skill, or getting something done to improve things, or just getting someone to listen. It will depend also on whether people discover that they can achieve by their own efforts something which is valued by others, and so come to believe in themselves.

References

1   *Concise Oxford Dictionary.*

2   A favourite word of R. S. Peters, who argues that worthwhileness derives 'from the character of the activities themselves'. Article 'In Defence of Bingo: A Rejoinder', *British Journal of Educational Studies*, Vol XV, 1967, p 191.

3   One recently described in writing his fellow-users as 'dossers, winers, down-and-outs, lay-abouts, drug abusers, meths drinkers and people of that nature'. He added that they should not be classed as animals, in the way that most people do: 'they don't think we also have brains'. In spite of this qualification, his statement produced angry reactions from some of the users. Also at The Kingsway are self-designated 'tramps', described by one of them as 'gentlemen of the High Road (or Low Road)', who live by casual jobs and despise those who 'doss' (which they link with the Dept of Social Security) and 'live from one hand-out to the next'.

4   Leaflet of the West End Co-ordinated Voluntary Services for Homeless Single People (WECVS), 57 Chalton Street, London NW1.

5   See Harold C. Wiltshire, 'The Concepts of Learning and Need in Adult Education', *Studies in Adult Education*, Vol 5, No 1, 1973, p 30: 'We dislike intensely the notion of being seen and seeing ourselves as "do-gooders", "manipulators" of other people – though this I believe is what, inescapably, we are.'

6   See Raymond Williams, *Culture and Society 1780–1950*, Penguin Books, 1958, Conclusion, pp 314–24.

7   The *Kingsway Herald*, December 1976, obtainable from the Training Unit, the City Lit, Stukeley Street, London WC2. Issue No 2 has appeared since.

8   CHAR, Campaign for Single Homeless People, 27 John Adam Street, London WC2.

9   The phrase comes from a comment of J. S. Bruner, *The Relevance of Education*, Penguin, p 120, where the author says that education should promote 'unpredictable services' in a technological world that could easily become 'alienated internally, flat emotionally and grey', by dealing with 'the range of things that increase the richness of individual response to other individuals'.

10   This is vividly reflected in the account of an art teacher, who for some weeks came into
      the centre to see what extension of activities she could stimulate. She describes one visit
      in this way:

      'I find the doorway, and there he is on the pavement, a bundle of old grey rags
      enfolding a fiery moon face, hand held out. One of my pupils? Not today. "Have you
      got a fag?" A smile and a quick dissent causes the molten eyelids to drop, the stance
      collapse, pathetic, hopeless ... Of what use am I to him? Every being with vitality has
      desires, everyone demands to be satisfied. It is a life force.... I do not know what it
      is to live without hope, never have I ceased to demand of the world. Here is a man for
      whom I have nothing, not even a cigarette.

      'And yet I have knowledge, he has experience. I am a teacher and must devise means
      to be effective. How can I give him hope, help him to feel he has power to improve his
      conditions? First I must get him a fag, then I must communicate in any way possible,
      talk, express in movement and gesture my liking and concern for him. Encourage him
      to do the same. He will then, like many others who only wait for the unfailing human
      contact, for continued uncompromising concern shown to them, give forth. Then we
      can begin. But what shall he express? His innermost needs, whether they be for past
      lost love, the exotic and exciting – or more simply a comfortable chair to sit on. Posters,
      paintings, ... what does it matter?' (Pat Turner.)

11   P. Freire, 'Extension or Communication', in *Education: The Practice of Freedom*, 9
      1973, Writers and Readers Co-operative, London.

12   Similarly it has been noted that the best theology is often done by lay people discussing
      human issues; but tell them they are doing theology and they stop immediately.

13   R. S. Peters, 'What is an Educational process?' in *The Concept of Education*, ed R. S.
      Peters, 1967, p 5.

14   The 'public' idea is stressed by K. H. Lawson, 'The Justification of Objectives in
      Adult Education', *Studies in Adult Education*, Vol 5, No 1, 1973. The negative effects
      of an educational monopoly are exposed by Ivan Illich, 'The Alternatives to Schooling',
      Saturday Review, 19 June 1971.

15   H. A. Jones, 'Education and Disadvantage', *Vaughan Paper 22* (Univ of Leicester Dept
      of Adult Education), 1977. And in 'A Rationale for Adult Education', in *Teaching
      Techniques in Adult Education*, ed Stephens and Roderick, 1971, p 191. He quotes
      the 1919 Report on adult education, which says that the mass of people need 'the
      development of an open habit of mind, clear-sighted and truth-loving, proof against
      sophisms, shibboleths, clap-trap phrases and cant'.

16   As J did: 'They gave me money and I drank the money because I was insulted. After
      that I spent eleven years in prison. I became a junky ... I had my pride.' Alcoholism,
      drugs, crime; just to show them!

17   Archie Hill, *A Cage of Shadows*, 1973, Hutchinson, London. 'Blokes like me are sort
      of unpaid professional victims – always in lumber, always at the receiving end.'

18   See the ending of Brecht's *Threepenny Opera*:

                        'Don't be too down on vice, for vice is cold
                        And freezes soon enough in its own frost
                        Think of the darkness and the bitter cold
                        That fills this shrieking valley of the lost.'

Clemence Dane compared this with Gay 'who dismissed his audience with a lollipop:
> But think of this Maxim, and put off your Sorrow,
> The Wretch of Today may be happy Tomorrow.'

Clemence Dane, *London Has a Garden*, Michael Joseph, London, 1964, pp 182–3.

19   The phrase comes from a pamphlet by Peter F. Conniff, *Homeless Single Men*, Bedfordshire Welfare Dept, 1966, where such a course is strongly advocated, but with little hope of success.

20   K is an example, who gives his surname as X, carries all his worldly possessions in the pockets of the numerous coats he wears, sleeps warm over a grating till moved on, and is a gentle man. He was not offered a paid cleaner's job at the centre because it was thought it would destroy him.

21   J. S. Bruner, *The Relevance of Education*, Penguin, p 170, who writes, 'In so far as a subculture represents a reaction to defeat, and in so far as it is caught by a sense of powerlessness, it suppresses the potential of those who grow up under its sway by discouraging problem solving.'

6

The Concept of Deprivation

R. W. K. PATERSON
(Studies in Adult Education, 6, 1974.)

The concept of 'deprivation' belongs to a cluster of concepts – 'deprived', 'underprivileged', 'disadvantaged' – which in recent years have played an increasingly large part in discussions of educational aims and policy. Sometimes these terms are used as if they all had the same meaning.[1] Sometimes they are used with scant regard to their literal meanings but with notable appreciation of their value as emotive weapons in the rhetorical campaigns of the day. Clearly it is of some moment for educators, including adult educators, to determine what such terms actually do mean, so that policy discussions can focus rigorously on the educationally significant issues and not meander indulgently off into the sands of verbiage. In what follows, therefore, I shall offer an analysis of the concept of deprivation which will, I hope, make plain in what ways this concept can, and in what ways it cannot, be used to crystallise issues in education, particularly certain issues facing contemporary educators of adults.

It will be obvious what these issues are. The debate about the universities' contribution to adult education in 'educational priority areas'; the alleged failure of the WEA to attract manual workers; the various proposals for conscripting adult education agencies in the service of schemes of 'community action'; the proposals that adult education agencies should practise 'positive discrimination' against 'privileged' students who study 'middle-class' subjects; the attempts to re-define the 'social purpose' of adult education in terms of our changed social attitudes and expectations: it is scarcely possible to discuss these issues without making reference, at every turn of the discussion, to those social groups who are described as 'educationally deprived', 'socially deprived', or deprived in some other way deemed to be relevant to the responsibilities and tasks of adult educators. The concept of deprivation figures right at the centre of contemporary concern in adult education. It links these central issues in adult education with wider educational, economic, and political issues involving questions of educational opportunity, economic equality, and social justice. As a concept it is expected to do a great deal of work in contemporary educational debate. Indeed, some writers seem to expect it to carry most of the burden of any argument they care to propound. However, like any other concept its range of application is finite, and it is surely desirable at the present time to consider just what its proper range of application is.

I shall begin by summarising the basic meaning of 'deprivation' as the term is used in ordinary discourse, for 'deprivation' *is* a term employed in ordinary discourse, not a technical term, and educators are under an obligation to use it in the generally understood ways. I shall then suggest three ways in which the concept of deprivation may be meaningfully applied within the domain of adult education – in other words, three main forms of educational deprivation suffered by adults. The third of these affects those adults who seldom or never avail themselves of the opportunities for liberal and recreational education of the kind provided, for example, by university extra-mural departments, the WEA, and local authority evening institutes. I shall refer to this kind of adult education as 'continuing lifelong education', and I shall next consider the types of evidence which are admissible, and the types of evidence which are not admissible, in determining whether some adult or group of adults is in fact deprived of continuing lifelong education in our society. Lastly I shall draw some conclusions concerning the theory and practice of adult education, which I believe follow from a correct analysis of the concept of educational deprivation.

Deprivation in General

The most general meaning of 'deprivation' is of course simply 'loss' or 'dispossession'. Naturally, what is lost is supposed to be worth having, since otherwise it would not be considered a 'loss'. What is lost may be a physical object, a faculty, a liberty, an appointment, a service, or any other kind of thing supposed to be valuable to the person deprived of it. It is *persons* who are deprived, although the concept may by analogical extension be applied even to insensate objects, as when one says that a plant is deprived of sunlight. And it is persons who *deprive*, although again by analogical extension we may say, for example, that a disease has deprived someone of the use of his limbs.

Since, as a matter of linguistic usage, that of which a person is deprived is *prima facie* valuable in some respect and to some degree, it must always be *prima facie* wrong to deprive anyone of anything. However, having acknowledged this, we must also acknowledge that this purely conceptual link between 'deprivation' and 'wrongfulness' does not take us very far. The *prima facie* case against deprivation *per se* is hardly a strong one, and is commonly overruled by moral considerations of weightier kinds. Clearly we cannot infer that an instance of deprivation is *ipso facto* an instance of injustice: that Smith is deprived of the opportunity to drive a car may be wrong, unjust, deplorable, or it may be entirely right, just, and laudable.

Nevertheless, in some contexts it is generally understood that the term 'deprived' stands for 'wrongly or unjustly deprived'. This is so, for example, when we speak of children who are deprived of affection. And in discussions of educational or social deprivation it is undoubtedly this elliptical, prescriptive usage which is in force. In such contexts to speak of deprivation is to speak of the *unjust* withholding of something to which, it is implied, the deprived parties are *entitled*, to which they have a *right* that is being denied. In discussing educational deprivation, then, we do not ask whether this or that instance is an instance of just or unjust deprivation, but simply whether it is an instance of deprivation or not really an instance of deprivation at all.

If it is an instance of deprivation, on the ground that some right of the deprived party is being denied, then of course the right in question may be either a legal right or a moral right. Rights in general are claims which society has a *prima facie* obligation to enforce, and if the right is a legal one it normally will be enforced, unless it clashes with some other right. However, if the right is a moral right not legally recognised, the most we can say is that it ought to be legally recognised, it ought to be enforceable, and the aim of reformers will be to gain legal recognition of it. We need not consider the various considerations which may give rise to rights: they may be deemed inherent in our nature as human beings, or in our membership of a given society, or they may arise as a result of some act or omission on our own part or that of others (marital rights, rights to compensation for injuries received, rights to payment for services rendered, and so on). We need only note, first, that a moral right must be enjoyed equally by all equals, that is, by all those satisfying whatever criteria are relevant for the enjoyment of the right, by all those persons who share the relevant circumstances or who display the relevant characteristics; secondly, that a moral right may be abrogated in whole or in part, if it conflicts with another right enjoyed by the same person or with a right enjoyed by some other person; and, lastly and most important of all, we must note that a right is a *discretionary* claim, entailing an absolute freedom on the part of the person enjoying it to exercise his right or not to exercise it, as he alone decides.

Educational Deprivation

In the light of the foregoing observations it will be apparent that 'educational deprivation' occurs when someone is being denied his right to education. But what precisely do we mean by a person's 'right to education'? Clearly we mean his right to be educated, but this phrase is not quite as simple as it sounds. The trouble is that the phrase, 'be educated', is systematically ambiguous. For a person to 'be educated' may mean that he is undergoing a certain process, that he is receiving education; or it may mean that he has attained a certain kind of status, that he has become in some degree an educated person. The term 'education' may signify an ongoing process, or it may signify a desirable achievement (resulting from that process). To say that Smith has a right to be educated, then, may mean that he has a right to participate in the educational process; or it may mean that he has a right to attain the status of an educated man. Accordingly, to say that Smith is educationally deprived may mean that he is being denied his right to a due participation in the educational process, or that he is being denied his right to become an educated man.

Now, I am very doubtful whether anyone could be said to have (and therefore ever to be denied) a right to education in the second sense I have distinguished. We cannot meaningfully be said to have a right to something, the attainment of which depends on our own efforts, and it is surely the case that the attainment (in whatever degree) of the mental status of an 'educated' person depends at least largely on the efforts of the person undergoing the educational process. No teacher can give a solemn guarantee of educational achievement to his students, since the achievement sought depends in large measure on the efforts of the students themselves. It is, therefore, in the first sense of 'education' that people can correctly be said to have a right to education. They have a right to a due share in the educational process, to a due share of the available opportunities, materials, and equipment, and to a due share of the knowledge, skills, sympathy, and patience of the available teachers. These are the educational resources at the disposal of society, and educational deprivation means the denial of one's right to a due share of these resources.

But what is a 'due share' of the available educational resources? It might be a share exactly equivalent to that assigned to every other member of society. Given differential student abilities, this would naturally result in widely differing degrees of educational attainment. Or it might be a share calculably sufficient to enable its recipient to reach some fixed degree of educational attainment which might be laid down as the educational norm for every member of society, a norm which the judicious redistribution of resources might ensure that everyone could reach and no one could surpass. Again, given differential student abilities, this criterion would produce marked differences between the shares of educational resources actually enjoyed by different individuals, the least able enjoying the greatest shares and the most able the smallest shares. Finally, the mode of distribution might be such as to ensure the maximisation of the educational attainments of the members of society taken as a whole, with resources being directed to those individuals likely to manifest the greatest increases in educational attainment. This classic utilitarian mode of distribution would be likely to result in both widely varying shares of the available educational resources and notably varying degrees of educational attainment.

I shall make no pretence of adjudicating among these alternative criteria of educational equity. Plainly, however, no discussion of educational deprivation can proceed without presupposing some conception of educational equity, and I may at least point out the imperative necessity of being quite clear about the type of educational equity presupposed before one ventures to mount complex arguments based on an appeal to the concept of deprivation. Let me simply state my own presuppositions, which I believe are fairly closely in line with the standards of educational equity tacitly endorsed by most concerned practitioners and observers in present-day Britain. It will then be possible to initiate a more direct examination of the issues facing adult education as a distinctive type of educational provision.

First, it seems to me that there is a definite, if fairly low, level of educational attainment which we can confidently expect most normal people to reach, even if their intellectual ability is meagre and their motivation poor, provided that we are determined to expend whatever educational resources may be necessary to ensure that most normal people in fact reach it. I am thinking of the moderate level of knowledge, and of physical, mental, and social skills, without which it is pretty well impossible for someone to lead a normal independent life in our society and to participate responsibly in its democratic processes. No doubt these minimal educational requirements rise as our social life becomes more complex, but I do not think many people would quarrel with the proposition that every member of society has a right to whatever share in the available educational resources may be necessary to ensure that he fulfils these requirements at any given period of time and at every point of his adult life. Let me call this the citizen's right to a 'basic general education'. An adult who has been denied his right to a basic general education is, then, suffering from one identifiable and grievous form of educational deprivation.

Second, I should want to maintain that every individual has a right (which comes into force once the universal right to a basic general education is satisfied) to a share of the remaining educational resources to be determined solely by his ability to profit from the processes of education. This share may be calculated on classic utilitarian principles of educational cost/effectiveness: if the educational benefit accruing to Brown from a given slice of the available educational resources exceeds the probable benefit accruing to Robinson, it is Brown who has a right to that slice – and to further slices until the law of diminishing returns establishes the final proportion holding between the two claimants. In this way (always within the limits of the resources available for this sector of educational provision) each individual may be deemed to have a right to an education which, in both extent and quality, accurately reflects his personal aptitudes and capacities. Let me call this his right to his 'formal personal education'. Anyone who has aspirations and talents unfulfilled that education might bring to fruition, at a time when educational resources are being wasted on those with neither talents nor aspirations, is a victim of injustice and is suffering from a second, although perhaps less easily identifiable, form of educational deprivation.

Third and last, I would postulate that, in a relatively wealthy society like ours at any rate, adequate provision is not being made for the educational rights of its members unless some portion of the available educational resources is set aside for 'continuing lifelong education', by means of which all adults, at any point of their lives and whatever their previous education, may explore fresh dimensions of experience and skill in the guided and systematic ways we call educational. An individual's due share of the resources set aside for continuing lifelong education is, I submit, a share exactly equivalent to that assigned to everyone else.[2] The purpose of continuing lifelong education is not to equip us with the basic essentials for social life; nor is it to superintend and direct the blossoming of our native aptitudes and capacities. Its purpose is, I think, simply to allow us to refresh and re-create ourselves, in a free and unencumbered spirit, at the common wellsprings of human culture. Thus the criteria of social responsibility and cost/benefit, which apply to basic general education and formal personal education respectively, do not apply to our rights in continuing lifelong education, and indeed there seems to be no valid criterion for assigning different rights to different individuals in this sphere. But if the principle of a simple and exact equality of rights is here the valid one, then we may conclude that anyone in our society who is denied a share of the resources available for continuing lifelong education equivalent to that enjoyed by everyone else is suffering from educational deprivation of the third and last kind I wish to distinguish.

Compensatory Education

If the foregoing account of what constitutes educational equity is accepted, it will be evident that those responsible for adult education in contemporary Britain may face three main kinds of educational deprivation, calling for three quite distinct concepts of provision. There may be, and there in fact are, otherwise normal adults who from one cause or another have not received the socially acceptable minimum of general education. There are also no doubt many adults, including some who have been educated to a high standard, who in some respects have not received the full measure of formal education by which they are capable of profiting. And there are adults who are denied access to their share of continuing lifelong education.

Three concepts of provision for educationally deprived adults need, then, to be distinguished. The first two will represent, in a clear sense, *compensatory* adult education. Basic compensatory education for the first group of the educationally deprived is to some extent undertaken by local education authorities (classes for illiterates, immigrants, etc) and could be undertaken by the WEA to a greater extent than it at present seems willing to do. Compensatory formal education for the second group needs to be undertaken by a variety of adult education agencies, operating at a variety of levels: the Open University, for example, is offering compensatory education at a high level for many persons who have been deprived of a formal university education. However, it should be emphasised that both of these first two groups are very heterogeneous. That they are distinct and characteristic groups of the educationally deprived certainly does not mean that they are distinct and coherent groups for teaching and administrative purposes. Nevertheless, it is important that both teachers and administrators should seek to identify and differentiate the members of these two groups, so that – albeit in many diverse ways – provision can be made for them which takes into account the degree of priority to which they are entitled. For surely the provision of compensatory adult education ought to enjoy some degree of priority over the provision of continuing lifelong education. In fact it seems fairly clear that basic compensatory education ought to be ascribed the very highest priority by adult educators, since until a man is equipped with certain basic skills (literacy, for example) and certain basic types of knowledge (some knowledge of the workings of society, for example) it is virtually impossible to discover and cultivate the distinctive talents and aptitudes he may have and therefore virtually impossible for him to enjoy his right to a formal personal education of a suitable kind; and it will be equally impossible for him to exercise his rights in continuing lifelong education.

Continuing Lifelong Education

However, it is to continuing lifelong education that I should now like to turn. Whatever proportion of the educational budget is set aside for this kind of adult education, certainly in an advanced society like our own some significant portion can be afforded, and arguably the educational progress of a society might be measured, not only by the total amount of resources devoted to education, but also by the proportion of educational resources which can be justly assigned to continuing lifelong education. Of the resources so assigned, each adult, I have claimed, is morally entitled to an exactly equal share. An adult who is denied his due share of the resources for continuing lifelong education is in this regard educationally deprived, and it is on this kind of deprivation that I now wish to concentrate, since it is this kind of deprivation which is of most direct concern to those engaged in liberal adult education in present-day Britain, and since the educational progress of society will increasingly make this by far the most widespread kind of educational deprivation.

What are the main types of evidence, then, which are relevant to establishing that a certain person or group of people is educationally deprived in this sense? Some writers seem to assume that the mere fact of a certain group's conspicuous and persistent absence from liberal and recreational adult classes in itself suffices to establish that the members of this group are suffering educational deprivation. Of course their failure to avail themselves of existing facilities is certainly a necessary piece of evidence in support of this proposition, but it hardly suffices to establish it, since of course their absence from adult education classes may be entirely voluntary. Where this is the case, education is not being *withheld*, it is being *refused* – and while this may be a lamentable state of affairs on many grounds, it is incorrect and deeply misleading to describe such people as 'deprived'.

In fact there are very many different causes, operating independently of the individual's will, which may make it very difficult for him to participate adequately in continuing lifelong education. Where one or more of these causes can be shown to operate, then there certainly does exist evidence – which may vary in quality from the watertight to the indirectly suggestive – that the individual in question is being deprived of his due share in continuing lifelong education. It is these verifiable and objectively operating causes for which the responsible adult educator ought to look if he is seeking evidence of deprivation.

Thus some people may be the victims of a political or administrative policy which effectively denies them equality of opportunity in adult education. In Britain this is unlikely to take the form of an act of injustice by commission (the deliberate exclusion of an individual or group from facilities otherwise generally available), although it may occur as injustice by omission (unequal provision by different local education authorities, for example, producing deprivation by geographical area).

Others may suffer from definite physical, social, or economic handicaps which make it extremely difficult for them to use the facilities generally provided. Old age, illness, physical disabilities, heavy family responsibilities, low income, lack of transport, overtime and shift working – the lives of many people are subject to these and other such circumscribing conditions, which obviously require to be carefully assessed when we are trying to establish the degree of remediable educational deprivation to be taken into account in a fair re-allocation of resources.

Still other people may be prevented from enjoying their due share of continuing lifelong education by specific educational handicaps of one kind or another. I am not thinking of defects in their basic general education or formal personal education (which are not relevant here); I am thinking of educational disabilities which are perfectly compatible with a good basic and even an advanced formal education but which may nevertheless disable certain people from following up interests which the facilities of continuing lifelong education exist to satisfy – for instance, a lack of knowledge of Greek or of the calculus, not previously felt as a lack until perhaps the person concerned finds himself unable to follow the course in theology or astronomy on which his adult interest centres.

Of course, a person's inability to participate fully in continuing lifelong education may result directly and foreseeably from his own voluntary and self-motivated actions. In such cases – while the disability or handicap is real enough – he himself is responsible for bringing it into being and it would be incorrect to describe him as 'deprived'. Heavy family commitments are often entered into willingly, and indeed often as a means to personal satisfaction; overtime and shift-working are often deliberately undertaken with the aim of acquiring an expensive car or enjoying a luxury holiday; the risk of imprisonment and its attendant restrictions is often deliberately accepted as part of the price of easy financial gain: in these and other cases the individual's rights to continuing lifelong education must be deemed to have been in some measure voluntarily waived, and it would be plainly unjust to put such cases in the category of the 'deprived' along with the many quite different cases of people (the elderly, the physically handicapped, and so on) whose disabilities have been incurred innocently and involuntarily.[3] Determining the degree of effective surrender of educational rights will be a difficult and complex task, and it almost always *will* be a matter of degree.

However, while there are no doubt many people whose educational disabilities are largely of their own making, there are certainly very many others who are undeniably deprived of continuing lifelong education by administrative, physical, social, economic, and educational causes over which they have little or no control. Again, of course, it will often be a matter of degree. There are those who are housebound because they were born crippled, and there are those who are housebound because they were crippled in an accident whilst driving on a motorway; one man works for weeks on end on a trawler because the alternative is unemployment, and another works for weeks on end on a trawler because the alternative is uprooting himself and his family. Although in the last three of these examples the cause of a possible educational disability results from an activity engaged in by the person liable to suffer it, we should I think nevertheless be prone to say that an educational disability produced by a cause of the kinds instanced could reasonably be accounted 'unavoidable' and the person suffering from the disability could be described with good reason as 'deprived'. Where a person suffers from an educational disability arising ultimately from some activity in which he has been engaged, I think that whether we are prepared to consider the disability 'unavoidable' and its sufferer 'deprived' depends, first, on the general *acceptability* of the activity in question (driving a car and working on a trawler are acceptable, burgling a house is not); secondly, on the degree of relevant *risk* normally attaching to the activity (the risk to one's opportunities of participating in adult education involved in driving a car is very low, the corresponding risk involved in begetting several children is fairly high); thirdly, on the degree of *awareness* of risk that might be reasonably expected of a normal person (anyone might be expected to know that working evening shifts would reduce his adult education opportunities, but we should not expect someone to know that moving from Loamshire to Chalkshire local education authority would have this effect); and lastly, on the range of *alternative* activities, not likely to produce educational disabilities, that might reasonably be considered to have been available to the person who is ostensibly deprived (there are few reasonable alternative jobs for a fifty-year-old Aberdonian trawlerman in a time of widespread unemployment, but there may be many reasonable alternatives for a cinema usherette in an area where there is an acute shortage of female labour for daytime jobs in shops and factories). In applying these criteria to determine whether and to what extent a person can really be held to be *deprived* of his due share of continuing lifelong education, we are often bound to find that there is much room for disagreement. But we are likely also to find many clear cases of genuine and serious deprivation which no one would dispute.

Now, it follows from everything I have said about educational equity that, where a case of *bona fide* deprivation has been established, the sufferer is entitled to educational redress, and the appropriate agencies of continuing lifelong education have a duty in strict justice to redistribute their resources accordingly. Everyone, I imagine, would agree that students prevented by educational handicaps not of their own making from pursuing specialised adult interests in astronomy, theology, and so on, should be given some measure of priority in adult education provision. Everyone would agree that some measure of priority should be given to the provision of continuing lifelong education, at suitable times and places and in suitable administrative frameworks, for trawlermen, the housebound, the elderly, the physically handicapped, and other individuals and groups whom adverse circumstances have in varying degrees prevented from enjoying the adult education facilities normally available to the general public. And when we say that such people have a right to their due share of the resources set aside for continuing lifelong education, we mean that it is their due share of the *educational* resources to which they have a right – teaching, books, equipment, and the rest – for inevitably it will often follow that, because of the higher costs involved in providing for many categories of the deprived, a larger share of the available *financial* resources will have to be expended if their just share of educational resources is to be adequately transmitted.

It seems highly probable that thorough empirical investigations would bring to light many different groups of people in every local authority and university extra-mural area who are deprived, usually by adventitious circumstances, of their rights in continuing lifelong education. There is little point in speculating in advance about the detailed outcome of such investigations.[4] But what we do need to settle in advance are the *kinds* of evidence which *count* as evidence of deprivation. I have suggested that, with some qualifications, the existence of verifiable and objective physical, economic, social, administrative, and educational barriers normally constitutes valid evidence of some ascertainable degree of deprivation. However, I should now like to consider one kind of evidence which is often adduced as evidence of deprivation but which, in my opinion, is very far from being evidence of anything of the sort.

The Abstainers

I refer to the attitudes of apathy and indifference which many people evince towards continuing lifelong education. There are very many people, of all social classes, in all age-groups, and at all educational levels, who are aware of the existence of opportunities for continuing lifelong education and are not prevented by any objective causes from availing themselves of these opportunities, but who nevertheless plainly demonstrate – in the most effective possible way, by total abstinence – that their rights in continuing lifelong education are a matter of complete indifference to them. Let me call these people 'the abstainers'. It is often claimed that the abstainers fall into the category of the deprived, and indeed that they may suffer from educational deprivation no whit less grievous than that suffered by the victims of more obvious physical, economic, or administrative causes.

Of course, *prima facie* this claim is absurd. It does not make sense to say that someone is deprived of something which is made available to him but which he rejects. If this usage of 'deprivation' were accepted, we should have to say that we were all 'deprived' of all the things we do not want and would not take if offered. However, those who advance the claim that the abstainers from continuing lifelong education are deprived naturally have no such absurd usage in mind, for of course what they in fact contend is that the *rejective attitude* of the abstainers is itself the product of disabling social, economic, or early educational causes over which the individual abstainer has little or no control and that the latter is for *this* reason in a very real sense deprived. Examples of psychologically disabling causes typically cited would be inadequate early schooling, damaging early experiences of formal education, the cultural impoverishment of working-class areas, or the cultural poverty of the early home environment.

I believe that this general claim, as it is commonly made, is false, or at best confused, for a whole variety of reasons, but I shall here confine myself to stating four criticisms which (I think) suffice to refute it.

In the first place, it is extremely doubtful whether a human being's attitudes and choices are the causal products of external social circumstances acting upon him. It is fashionable to suppose that this must be so, but unfashionable to think carefully about what this supposition logically involves. While I have no wish to deny the manifest connection between social circumstances and the attitudes and choices of individuals, those who assert that the connection is *causal* are surely guilty of an immense oversimplification. The connection between human choices and their external antecedents is quite unlike the connection between the boiling point of a liquid and the external atmospheric pressure or any other *bona fide* case of strictly causal connection. Unlike physical objects, human beings perceive, interpret, and evaluate the circumstances operating upon them; their ensuing attitudes and choices are *responses to* these circumstances, not simple *resultants of* them. But if a man's rejection of educational opportunities is not a simple causal product of his social and early educational background; if, that is to say, he himself as a conscious choosing being is responsible for *forming* his rejective attitudes (formed in the face of, but not 'as an unavoidable result of', his particular circumstances); then it is, to say the least, highly misleading to suggest that he suffers from a 'psychological disability' comparable to the unavoidable physical, social, or economic disabilities of others in the light of which, we have seen, they are justly considered to be deprived.[5]

Secondly, it cannot be too clearly emphasised that a true cause is *always* followed by its effect. Whenever a putative cause is not followed by its putative effect, this shows either that we were mistaken in considering that it was the true cause of the effect in question or (more probably) that the putative 'cause' was only an element in the overall cause, the other elements in which we then proceed to seek. Now, many people who have had inadequate early schooling or who come from culturally impoverished homes nevertheless avail themselves of educational opportunities in later life, and thus (even if we accept that it makes sense to speak of the 'causes' of human attitudes) it is evidently false to assign any of these factors as the cause of the rejective attitude of the abstainers. If it is fashionable to regard such factors as causative, this is because it is simply assumed that the abstainers' attitude *must* be caused and that therefore other, undiscovered elements in their social or educational background *must* be operating in combination with the factors on which chief focus is directed. Even if this latter assumption were true, these other, hypothetical, undiscovered elements might be events within the control of the abstainers and so might not constitute evidence in favour of the claim that they are deprived; but in any case the assumption in question is no more than a deterministic act of faith until it receives substantiation from subsequent research, which would have to identify a set of social factors followed in *every* case by a rejective attitude to adult educational opportunities. No such empirical substantiation is ever received. If, notwithstanding this, the original claim is still advanced, this is because it is really grounded on the *metaphysical* premise of psychological determinism. Those who claim that rejection of adult educational opportunities signifies educational deprivation are, then, ultimately basing their claim, not on empirical data as they profess, but on a covert appeal to the undemonstrated metaphysical theory that each and every human attitude and choice is the pre-determined outcome of ineluctably operating causes.

In the third place, even if we were to allow that it made literal sense to speak of human attitudes and choices being caused and indeed were to allow that it was true to describe all human attitudes and choices without exception as the predetermined results of rigidly operating causes, the general claim we are considering would – because of these very assumptions – have logical corollaries which would seriously embarrass its supporters. For it would prove that *every* abstainer (not merely those with poor social or educational backgrounds) was a case of educational deprivation. Since the determinist claims that the life-situation of Darby and Joan Hodge in the cottage is the cause of their indifference to their adult educational opportunities, he is bound to acknowledge that the life-situation of the Duke and Duchess of Omnium in the castle is the cause of *their* indifference to their adult educational opportunities: the social and psychological causes at work are very different but fully as causative, the end-result is the same and the psychological disablement is just as complete. In practice, however, the determinist makes no attempt to be consistent. Considering abstinence as a sign of 'deprivation' in the case of miners, dockers, or factory workers, he considers it a sign of 'philistinism' in the case of stockbrokers, landlords, and company directors.

In practice he adheres to the arcane metaphysical theory that causes cease to be truly causative somewhere above £3,000 per annum.

Fourth and last, the assumption that our educational attitudes and choices are the causal products of social and other conditions is incompatible with a belief in educational *rights*. The concept of a 'right' is the concept of a *discretionary* claim, one which we may or may not decide to exercise, as we alone freely choose. If all our educational choices are the causal products of antecedent circumstances (the positive choices of those who avail themselves of continuing lifelong education, be it noted, no less than the negative choices of the abstainers), then the concept of a genuinely free choice to participate or not to participate in continuing lifelong education simply becomes inapplicable; and of course with it the concept of a genuinely discretionary claim, a *right* properly so called to continuing lifelong education, becomes inapplicable also. But someone is said to be 'deprived' of continuing lifelong education only if his 'right' to continuing lifelong education is being denied. The argument that people are deprived of continuing lifelong education because social and other factors have caused them to reject existing opportunities leads, then, to the absurd conclusions that strictly speaking people do not have 'rights' to continuing lifelong education, that consequently they have no rights to be *denied*, and that therefore denial of their educational rights or educational deprivation cannot ever be correctly said to occur.

Implications for Adult Education

The foregoing analysis has, I believe, wide-ranging implications for the theory and practice of adult education, and by way of conclusion I shall make brief reference to some of the most obvious of these.

It should be evident that it is deeply unwise to base inferences concerning educational deprivation solely or mainly on the fact that the members of this or that social group tend not to avail themselves of existing provision. In a free society people of all classes have the right to settle their own leisure priorities, and while professional adult educators may look askance at scales of priority in which adult educational activity does not figure, we ought not to undervalue them or treat them as less freely and responsibly arrived at than our own: we must take the priorities of others seriously, even and especially when they are not in accord with our own. A man's rights in continuing lifelong education are discretionary claims, which he may or may not exercise, as he alone chooses. The mentality which frames adult education policies designed to ensure that everyone will in fact exercise his rights is a mentality which either does not grasp or does not respect the notion of genuine educational rights. It may mask its paternalism behind talk of educational 'needs', but the concept of a need, while a valid and important one when put to its proper uses, cannot be used to settle questions concerning deprivation of continuing lifelong education, which are settled only by appeal to the concept of *rights*. Men have rights to many things which they cannot be said to *need*, and continuing lifelong education (unlike basic general education) clearly cannot be described as a necessity of normal living. In any case, if we judge that we have an obligation to satisfy people's proven needs, this is surely because the concept of a 'need' is the concept of a lack which the sufferer has a *right* to have remedied. Thus it is always ultimately by reference to rights that the concept of deprivation requires us to offer educational redress, and we have seen that it is logically and morally impossible to ensure that the rights will always be in fact exercised or the redress accepted.

Another area in which misuse of the concept of deprivation may lead to deep confusion is that of adult education and social class. The question of provision for manual workers, for example, is distinct from the question of provision for the educationally deprived; they raise distinct though overlapping sets of issues, and only confusion can result from treating the two questions as if they were identical. It would be fallacious for the WEA to assume that it could discharge its special responsibilities in the sphere of working-class education by making special provision for the educationally deprived, or that it could provide adequately for the deprived by focusing its efforts on provision for the working-class. The concept of 'the working-class' is extremely vague, but we may at least be sure that it is not identical with the concept of 'the educationally deprived'. In so far as the term retains any clear meaning, 'the working-class' is largely defined by its valuations, including the relatively low value which it sets on adult education (a valuation which adult educators must respect, while of course dissenting from it), and there is certainly no reason to suppose that this vast, amorphous group of people suffers homogeneously from some inclusive form of economic, physical, or early educational deprivation. No doubt many individuals and sub-groups of the working-class are seriously deprived of opportunities for continuing lifelong education (the elderly, for example), and no doubt declining standards in State primary and secondary schools could eventually result in large numbers of working-class people suffering from serious deprivation in respect of their basic general education and formal personal education. However, individuals and sub-groups of 'the middle-class' also suffer deprivation of continuing lifelong education, from much the same causes, and the great majority of middle-class children are also vulnerable to deprivation from declining standards in State schools. Thus the idea of a campaign of 'positive discrimination' against middle-class students in continuing lifelong education, perverse and offensive because of its undertones of vindictiveness, is doubly perverse because the vindictiveness is misplaced. Middle-class people frequently choose to exercise their educational and cultural rights, and indeed it is partly because of this that they are styled 'middle-class'. But it is confused to describe middle-class adult students as therefore 'privileged' in some homogeneous and inclusive sense, and false to suggest that special provision is made for them by arranging courses in 'middle-class subjects'. Our students, of whatever class, are those adult members of the community who voluntarily enrol on courses normally arranged because the subjects of study are objectively judged by the providing agencies to be educationally worthwhile in their own right. Indeed, to the extent that middle-class people are more educationally oriented and to the extent that educationally oriented people have more varied and definite educational interests, to that extent middle-class people are if anything *more* likely to suffer from deprivation, since the range of subject provision in continuing lifelong education is always of necessity limited in any given locality.

Finally, it is worth emphasising that, imperative as is our duty to make full and prompt provision for the educationally deprived, such provision must be seen for what it is – an exercise in educational redress, not an instrument of social change. It is of course to be expected that the laudable concern for social justice which animates many teachers and organisers in adult education will be the motivating force which leads some of them to work with the educationally deprived, and of course it would be very surprising if social changes of some sort did not ensue as a result of their work. These social changes might be desirable or undesirable (it is too lightly assumed that they will be uniformly desirable), but whatever their character they cannot make our educational responsibility to the deprived any greater or less an obligation, for in itself it is already an obligation of the most stringent kind. It is a duty in educational equity, that is, in the strictest sense of educational justice, and it therefore admits of no diminution or partial fulfilment. However, it is an *educational* duty. We have a duty to those who are deprived of continuing lifelong education – in literature, the arts, history, philosophy, the sciences, languages, and crafts – and this duty is not fulfilled by providing socially useful courses of non-educational kinds, valuable though these may be on other grounds. Courses on welfare rights or on the organisation of pre-school playgroups, for example, may sometimes meet real needs, and may even have some educational content, but it would be a gross dereliction to regard such courses, however widely organised or enthusiastically supported, as contributing except in the most meagre and indirect ways to redressing the educational deprivation which, as adult *educators*, it is our distinctive responsibility to amend. This responsibility may be, and ought to be, discharged in diverse ways by diverse agencies, operating in their appropriate spheres, and at appropriate levels of work. But for all of us it is a paramount responsibility, and it is accordingly paramount to recognise its nature and define its limits, lest in the end we fail through an excess of zeal and a want of lucidity.

References

1   The Russell Report, which will no doubt help to focus attention on educational deprivation, prefers to employ the concept of 'the disadvantaged'. See para 277, which refers to 'our particular concern for the disadvantaged'. It eschews formal definition of this term, giving instead a list of specimen cases of 'the disadvantaged' (while not claiming that these specimen cases are in any way representative). Perhaps as a result, it becomes possible to speak of 'deprivation' and 'disadvantage' as if these terms were synonymous: eg para 282, where 'social deprivation' is said to be 'often associated with other disadvantage'. In fact, however, someone may be at a disadvantage without being in the least deprived: the amiable grasshopper is not deprived, but when winter comes he is at a considerable disadvantage compared with the industrious ant.

2   In respect of continuing lifelong education this goes further than the letter (if not the spirit) of the Russell Report, which defines 'equality of educational opportunity' (at para 58.1) as 'equality of opportunity for each individual to benefit, *according to his personal capacities*, from the total range of educational provision' (my italics).

3   See the Russell Report, para 58, for a tendentious juxtaposition of the inmates of hospitals and prisons – as if burglary, for example, were comparable to an illness with which essentially innocent people could be smitten. However, the Report is admittedly here speaking of 'the disadvantaged', manifestly not the same category as 'the deprived'. An imprisoned safebreaker is certainly at a disadvantage, compared say with a housewife, for attending courses in marine biology; but it would be misleading to describe him as 'deprived' in this respect.

4   See Peter Clyne, *The Disadvantaged Adult* (Longmans, 1973), for an outline of an investigation into some types of educational deprivation and other kinds of educational handicap.

5   The Russell Report, in speaking of educational disadvantages, refers (para 279) to 'isolation from the messages of educational agencies through ignorance or rejection of the imagery and vocabulary they use', as if 'ignorance' and 'rejection' were essentially similar kinds of mental state or as if a rejective attitude to continuing lifelong education could only be based on ignorance.

7

Adult Education and Social Change

J. E. THOMAS AND G. HARRIES-JENKINS
(Studies in Adult Education, 7, 1975.)

In any analysis of the relationship between adult education and social change, a major methodological problem is the absence of a conceptual framework within which discussion can take place. One effect of this can be seen in the debate about the legitimacy of educational objectives. It is apparent that conclusions which are put forward assume a theoretical priority of some specific set of variables – economic, technological, ecological, ideological or normative. The stress which is placed on the perceived importance of one of these then produces conclusions which range from the argument that social change must be totally repudiated as an educational aim,[1] to the assumption that social change is a legitimate and central aim of adult education.[2] When these conclusions are considered further, however, it is clear that they form, together with the 'middle point of view', part of a continuum which reflects variations in individual attitudes towards the legitimacy of postulated aims. In turn, the continuum is a major component of a conceptual framework which seeks to link attitudes with the activities which are carried on as part of the adult education curriculum.

The Continuum of Attitudes

The continuum, it is suggested, is based on two important and interrelated factors which account for the attitudes of adult educationalists and their concept of the relationship between adult education and social change. First, it is based on two interpretations of social interests. These approximate to a *conflict* and *consensus* view, respectively, of society. Conflict theorists approach the question of social change from the standpoint of the interests of the various individuals and groups within society. The needs and desires of these factions, rather than the needs of society as a whole, motivate their attitudes towards the division of power and privilege.[3] Essentially, these theorists see social inequality as arising out of the struggle within society for valued goods and services in short supply. They emphasise the effects of domination, exploitation and coercion, concluding that a central objective of adult education must be the production of changes in a society's basic outlook and goals.

Consensus theorists, in contrast, approach the problem of social interests from the viewpoint of society as a whole. The interests of society are then seen to be compatible with the best interests of the individual, for it is the needs of the latter, as part of the whole, which govern the needs and requirements of the total social system. The cohesion, stability, and performance of this consensus model therefore emphasise not the struggle for power and privilege but the significance of norms and behavioural standards which are seen to be the basic elements of social life. To these theorists, adult education is not a facility for promoting the social policies of a particular group, but is a means of transmitting the inherited knowledge and culture of the whole society. Value-judgements are then concerned with cognitive rather than social or political values.

Despite the widespread criticism in the recent literature of social theory of these two models of society,[4] both theories have a particular relevance in the analysis of the relationship between adult education and social change. The nature of group interests, as they are interpreted by supporters of the conflict model of society, suggests that to the mature student, education is seen as a means whereby the power, prestige and privilege of the group can be increased. More importantly, the identification of this model with the proposition that social systems are dynamic, encourages the belief that adult education is an important vehicle of change. The concept of adult education as a radical force, seeking to make a major impact on society, suggests that an education programme is only valid or viable if it seeks to challenge basic assumptions about socio-economic structures, value systems and cultural or aesthetic norms. There is a total rejection of any interpretation of the objectives of adult education which identifies its goals with the maintenance of the existing social system.

Supporters of the consensus model, however, tend to believe that adult education has no role as an instigator or supporter of change. Society in the form of its existing structures, value-systems and norms, is accepted as a framework within which the activities of adult education can be carried out. From this point of view, it is not the primary task of adult education to challenge the validity of this framework, although such a challenge *may* arise as a concomitant of the transmission of knowledge and culture. If such a challenge does not occur, this does not reduce the intrinsic value of a devised teaching programme, for the essential question is whether the transmitted knowledge has been educationally worthwhile.

In addition to the effect of this consensus/conflict interpretation of social interest on attitudes towards the relationship between adult education and change, a second determinant of attitudes is the distinction between value-oriented and norm-oriented perceptions. This distinction has been clearly brought out by Smelser who has shown how a value-oriented organisation is directed towards changes in the generalised ends or values that a social order is designed to achieve. Conversely, a norm-oriented organisation seeks to retain existing goals although it aims to change the rules that govern the *pursuit* of basic objectives and the detailed operation of basic forms of social order.[5] The contrast is between revolution and reform and in this context the role of adult education is of critical importance. By themselves, for example, values and norms do not determine who will be agents in the pursuit of valued ends, or how the action of these agents will be structured into concrete roles and organisations. It is the 'mobilisation of motivation into organised action' which is of fundamental significance, and here adult education is of importance for two reasons. In the first place, it provides the *structure* by which this mobilisation can be achieved, creating a community of association which exercises moral, intellectual and, if needed, forcible control over the society which supports it. In some ways it has a role which has been termed that of the 'secular church'[6] for where it is value-oriented, the purpose of the community is seen to be that of 'meditating' on the state of society and of then promoting change. In contrast, the importance of the structure, where it is norm-oriented, is derived from the cybernetic role of adult education.[7] Here, the perceived responsibility for conserving and elaborating the higher cultural standards of society ensures that adult education organisations exercise a form of control whereby the criteria of normative standards are applied in the solution of contemporary problems.

In addition to providing the structure for the mobilisation of motivation, adult education is of importance because it creates the *situational facilities* which are a major component of social action. These facilities are the means and obstacles which facilitate or hinder the attainment of declared goals in the organisational context, and it is knowledge of the opportunities and limitations in society which are critical determinants of behaviour. This second reason for the apparent significance of adult education as the creator of an environment which is conducive to the promotion of change has lengthy historical antecedents. Its applicability, for example, can be seen in a statement made by Tawney in 1914:

> *The first task of any such society as the Workers' Educational Association is to lay to rest that smiling illusion which whispers that 'culture' is something which one class – the educated – possess, that another – the 'uneducated' – are without.*[8]

Consistently, this belief that the primary aim of adult education is to promote the development of situational facilities, has been endorsed by writers in this area. The writings of Maurice, Tawney, Mansbridge and Cole, for example, repeatedly stress how the student's knowledge of the opportunities and limitations of the environment and his own knowledge of his abilities to influence the environment are important determinants of his attitudes. In short, his knowledge is related directly to the possibility of achieving a goal which is part of his role or part of his conception of the importance of adult education as a means of social change.

On the basis of these two factors, that is, the relationship between a conflict and consensus model of society, and the contrast between value- and norm-orientations, we can identify a continuum of attitudes which is of essential importance in the further understanding of the complex relationship between adult education and social change. The distinction between attitudes is rarely expressed, in practice, in terms of the polar extremes which have been suggested. The concept of adult education as a radical force, primarily seeking to make a major impact on society, or as a conservative force devoted to the atomistic view of man is, in everyday life, subject to considerable constraints. These concepts are, therefore, best seen as part of a continuum. At one extreme, we are dealing with the view that any system of adult education *must*, if it is to be effective, challenge established economic, political and social assumptions. At the other, we encounter the argument that adult education should only be concerned with the conservation of traditionally accepted normative standards. Between these two positions, there are a number of less extreme views which recognise that while there may be inevitable social and political concomitants of all educational activities, there is a spectrum of legitimate educational aims in which some are closer to the management of social change and others closer to the conservation of inherited cultural traditions.

The Theoretical Framework

When these attitudes are analysed, it can be suggested that interpretation of the relationship between adult education and social change can be grouped under four categories:

Revolution   Reform   Maintenance   Conservation

The characteristics of each of these shade into those of its neighbour on a continuum of attitudes and interpretations, but each group displays certain distinct and peculiar features. Thus the characteristics subsumed under the heading of *revolution* are essentially derived from the conflict model of society and the value-oriented interpretation of the function of adult education. These are primarily individual or group-oriented, so that one criticism of this position is that it emphasises the 'inflamed ambition of individuals'.[9] An interesting corollary of this criticism is that it identifies 'revolution' with an inherent radicalism and that this association seems to be generally accepted. It must be noted, however, that a belief in a justified social revolution need not be exclusively 'radical' in character. As Barrington Moore has pointed out, revolution can also emanate from 'above'.[10] In this respect, adult education can be used as a vehicle for encouraging or endorsing a fascist revolution through the conscious manipulation of the public mind so as to create, as in Germany during the 1930s, ready acceptance of postulated ideological doctrines.[11] In both cases, however, adult education, irrespective of the precise political connotation which can be associated with this concept of revolution, continues to be identified with ideas of individual or group advantage.

Although this concept is in no way a new phenomenon, it is noticeable that it is no longer interpreted simply as a specific concept concerned only with political events and goals. Instead, it has become an unstructured concept representing an idealised pattern of social relationships. The idea of violence, unpredictability, the overthrow of the powerful, resistance to domination, and independence remained. But in the new synthesis revolution was much more. It was youth defying age, liberation from the population explosion and social constraints, achieving the impossible, a formula for re-shaping the world in any image, internal or external.[12] This, then, is the revolution of social engineering or social upheaval. It is Emerson's 'do your own thing'[13] or Johnson's a 'millenarian rebellion',[14] situations in which the objectives of adult education programmes are seen to be the need to challenge basic assumptions about society, and the need to encourage stasis or social dissolution.

In contrast with this contemporary interpretation of the nature of revolution, the concept of *reform* seems to be more closely linked with an historical past. While it too is concerned with changes within society, many of its characteristics are reminiscent of comments which were made in the nineteenth century. It would be incorrect to identify the concept solely with those early theories of social revolution, but this interpretation of the relationship between adult education and society owes a great deal to the nineteenth-century model. Paine's defence of the French Revolution, for example, remains a very apt comment on this concept of reform. It is, in his words, 'a renovation of the natural order of things, a system of principles as universal as truth and the existence of man, and combining moral with political happiness and national prosperity'.[15] Indeed, in many ways, the movement for reform can be seen 'not as the initiative of a new age, but as the last formula of an expiring age'.[16]

In adult education circles, this concept of reform is a very popular one. It is attractive, for example, to those liberals who, while they reject the validity of the consensus model of society, are not prepared to endorse a revolutionary appeal for total social dissolution. It continues to be based on an awareness of individual or group interests, but these are now interpreted as a complex symbiotic relationship between members of interest groups. The latter possess 'affinities of interest', arising from sources as diverse as 'relations of kinship, the division of labour, exchanges in the market place, and the ubiquitous influence of custom'.[17] The interest groups which are thereby formed reflect the differences in their goals. Political parties, the military, business groups, trade unions, and organised pressure groups are all representative of an amorphous power structure.

The attraction of these groups to adult educationists is derived from a realisation that these groups are dynamic rather than static. Adult education can then be clearly seen to have a purpose. On the one hand, it can press for reforms in the structure of these groups, using adult education programmes as a social dynamic while not challenging the assumptions which legitimise the existence of these groups. Alternatively, it can prepare students for membership of these groups, preparing them for the exercise of social duties and responsibilities, and encouraging their educational and social mobility. These groups are also attractive because they can be conceptualised as *veto-groups*, each of which is primarily concerned with protecting its jurisdiction by blocking the action of other groups which seem to threaten it.[18] This interpretation minimises the effect of conflict, in the sense that conflict can be defined as the elimination of an opposition to achieve a given goal, and substitutes instead the idea of competition. Once again, this gives a sense of purpose to adult education programmes. Life can now be seen to be 'a series of hurdle-jumps, the hurdles of scholarships which are won by learning to amass and manipulate the new currency'.[19] The principles of competition, the idea of the career open to talent, and the desire to create a just open society, emphasise the value of the contribution which adult education can make to the development of individual personality.

Popular endorsement of the merits of this reform movement is not based, however, simply on the attractiveness of the theory of interest groups. In Great Britain, the demand for reform has a lengthy history and it has been encouraged in a wide variety of situations. While the concept of revolution is primarily associated with political movements and ideologies, that of reform is much more widely based. The latter can be seen, for example, in the traditions of Christian democracy for which Mansbridge stood in the WEA. Out of the alliance of the adult schools and the Quakers, there stemmed the educational settlements[20] with their own theories of reforming the insular, the sectarian and the personal.[21] This stirring of the social conscience was echoed, particularly in the years between 1919 and 1939, in a wide number of other educational institutions. The tragedy of much of this reform movement, however, was that somewhere along the way it lost direction. Too much time was spent in debating problems of organisation or administration, too little time was spent in considering the need to relate contemporary social developments to traditional areas of concern.[22]

One effect of this was to blur the boundaries between the *reform* and the *maintenance* interpretation of the relationship of adult education to society. In theory, there are important distinctions between these two interpretations. The concept of reform is based on a conflict theory of society, whereas the concept of maintenance draws its inspiration from the opposing consensus model. In practice, however, it may be difficult to identify the particular characteristics which are usually attributed to the two models in question. This can be seen in a number of examples. Supporters of the reform concept thus argue that their primary concern is with society as a whole, not the interests of any specific group, although the reform/conflict thesis is essentially based on the idea of sectional interests. Conversely, the maintenance concept, theoretically based on the needs of society as a whole, may be interpreted to mean the wish to create a stable society for the continuing advantages of particular interests or groups.

The second example is perhaps more important. Consensus, it is argued, does not necessarily mean persistence as opposed to change. There may be, as Cohen has pointed out, 'consensus on the direction and forms of change'.[23] Similarly, the absence of consensus or the placing of an undue emphasis on the interests of a particular group, may create a dysfunctional situation which, through the emergence of an impasse, prevents or inhibits planned change. A final example emphasises the theoretical difficulties which occur. The concept of maintenance is based on the idea of social integration, relying on the consensus, solidarity or cohesion which are characteristics of the consensus model of society. But, as Lockwood argues, integration may well be applicable to societies with structured conflict, since the latter ensures the functional interrelationship of the various parts of the social structure.[24] In this sense, therefore, the idea of integration cannot be regarded as an exclusive characteristic of the maintenance/consensus model, since it may be found in the reform/conflict model.

Although the difficulty of reconciling these criticisms with the postulated characteristics of the two models of society is very evident in the extensive literature on the subject, it is important to remember that the creation of the models owes a great deal to ideology.[25] For the adult educationist, therefore, their importance is derived not from their methodological correctness, but from the reasoned ideological arguments which underlie the defence of either or both of the two models. One effect of this is that the concept of maintenance, as it is interpreted by the supporters of this idea of the relationship between adult education and society, is associated with a wish to maintain the existence of those norms which are considered to be the basis of social life. They are particularly involved in the maintenance of the underlying system of values which influence the norms to be found throughout society. There is thus ample evidence of a developed interest, not only in ensuring a sense of commitment to those norms, but also in creating consensus on the values which produce them. The most suitable situation for ensuring the development of adult education programmes orientated to these ends is found, it is believed, in a stable social system which encourages the maintenance of the *status quo*. Here, the formulation of societal goals in terms of the accepted norms, and the creation of a harmonious sense of values, encourage the creation of teaching programmes which are specifically designed to encourage social integration.

The possibility of change is not excluded from consideration. To be accepted as valid, however, this must be a planned change which arises as society, as a whole, adapts to universally accepted amendments to existing norms and values. Changes which are reflections of sectional interests are disregarded, on the grounds that these do not contribute towards the maintenance of the whole. A resulting preoccupation with the believed needs of society can be discerned in most discussions about the role of adult education in relation to socio-cultural factors. Among these, for example, a frequent cause of controversy arises from the postulated need to produce a large number of educated specialists who can fill appointments as administrators, professionals and managers. It is here that the liberal versus vocational argument is most frequently pursued, although the force of the arguments used are weakened by the general agreement that there is a need to achieve a synthesis between the two conceptions of a literary or technical culture.

A second special need which, it is argued, can be filled through the medium of adult education programmes, is the requirement of society for 'productive workers who enjoy their lives. This means the most economical and effective use of manpower, and it also means that happiness is a factor in efficiency'.[26] The implications of this as an educational goal are far-reaching. For many employers of labour, it endorses their belief in a custodial model of organisational behaviour, in which the natural measure of morale is employee satisfaction.[27] Consequently, they approve or support adult education activities which contribute to the development of employee maintenance needs and increase the latter's organisational dependency. Concomitantly, they reject the validity of courses which are based on the premises of reform or revolution, and in certain circumstances, the employer can actively oppose the establishment or continuation of 'radical' adult education programmes.[28]

A belief that this goal of individual happiness is best satisfied in the maintenance model through programmes which are based on established norms and values creates several problem areas. A bipartite system of adult education may be created in which 'recreational' programmes designed to promote a general liberal education, are sharply distinguished from 'reparative' or 'renovative' courses.[29] It is disputed whether these latter courses properly fall within the province of the university extra-mural department and the established bodies. At the same time, 'liberal' is narrowly defined to exclude many of the courses which are held in evening institutes, so that the concept of happiness or social needs is interpreted to mean these concepts, as they are interpreted by the educational élite. Indeed, the very idea of maintenance tends to assume that it is only an élite who can best judge the type of education which is required to ensure the continued stability of society. As a result, maintenance may be tutor- rather than student-oriented, for individual requirements, it is argued, must be subordinated to the believed needs of society, and to the need to maintain standards.

The emphasis which is placed in the maintenance model on the stability of society is carried a stage further in the conservation model, for here there is a total rejection of change. Whereas it is accepted in the maintenance model that planned change may be a necessary corollary of stability, conservationists adopt an ultra-conservative stance which is opposed to any association of adult education with changes within society. This includes the rejection of any courses which may be defined as renovative, that is, designed to retrain qualified individuals, as well as courses which can be more directly associated with reform or revolution. In the conservation model, the aims of adult education are seen as the need to protect the traditional subjects of study from change, and the need to uphold an élite tradition in education.

The justification for the retention of this model is largely based on conceptions of education as something which is gentlemanly, non-utilitarian and largely ornamental. The goal of this model was admirably summed up by T. S. Eliot when he wrote that 'The first task of the communities should be the preservation of education within the cloisters uncontaminated by the deluge of barbarism outside'.[30] Eliot, however, was not alone in his interpretation of the goals of education, and a common theme among adult educationists who are supporters of the conservation model is their dislike of a contemporary 'mechanized, commercialized, industrialized existence'.[31]

The arguments which have been used to justify the existence of this model have been admirably analysed by Flann Campbell, although it would be incorrect to interpret his comments on 'Latin and the Elite Tradition in Education'[32] to mean that the conservationist in adult education is only concerned with the teaching of classics. His analysis of the élite tradition in education shows how, apart from the linguistic and aesthetic aspects of the classics, this tradition is oriented towards the identification of education with training for leadership. From this doctrine, and on the basis of the faculty theory of psychology which claimed that what was important in teaching a subject was not so much interest or relevance but formal training and mental discipline, 'flowed the theory that in adult life the liberally educated amateur was to be preferred to the vocationally-trained specialist'.[33] Accordingly, the conservation model in adult education continues to emphasise the need for courses which encourage the acquisition of mental skills. The important feature of this interpretation is that the conservationist believes firmly in the existence of two cultures or, rather, in the existence of an 'educated man's culture' which only a small part of the population are capable of appreciating or acquiring, and the 'culture of the rest'. Consequently, it is argued, it is only an educated élite who can participate in these areas of adult education and the élite, by definition, must be closed to the greater part of the student body as a whole.

In rejecting the need for social change, the supporters of this model thus consistently reiterate the importance of adult education as the guardian of traditional standards, norms and value. The barbarians, in Eliot's words, are at the gate and to prevent their entry barriers based on scholarship, on the existence of only one legitimate culture and on the rejection of all but a small number of subjects as suitable for study, must be raised. The extent to which this interpretation of adult education can be seen as 'legitimate' is questionable, but it must be recognised that the attitudes which are subsumed under this heading are a reflection of particular evaluations of the relationship between adult education and social change, and it is this evaluation which ultimately characterises the potential validity of the postulated continuum.

The model of attitudes which has been outlined here can be considerably developed to take into account such factors as curriculum content, appropriate methods of knowledge transmission, student motivation and so on. Its usefulness as a conceptual tool is thus not limited to the analysis of attitudes towards the role and function of adult education as a change agent. Nevertheless it is in this area that its initial applicability helps us understand the reaction of individuals and groups to any postulated thesis concerning the legitimacy of educational objectives. Polarised points of view may be rarely encountered, but the distinction between the reform and maintenance positions is frequently encountered in discussions about the duty of adult education, about its course content and about the allocation of resources. The importance of the model, therefore, is that it enables us to understand the broad spectrum of proffered opinions, and that it encourages our appreciation of, if not our agreement with, aims which our colleagues are seeking to achieve in this area of study.

References

1   R.W.K. Paterson, 'Social change as an educational aim', in *Adult Education*, vol 45, no 6, 358.
2   Cf K. Jackson and T. Lovett, 'Universities and the WEA – an alternative approach', in *Adult Education*, vol 44, no 2.
3   Cf Gerhard Lenski, *Power and Privilege* (New York, 1966), 16–17.
4   Cf Percy Cohen, *Modern Social Theory* (London, 1968), 166–7.
5   Neil J. Smelser, *Theory of Collective Behaviour* (New York, 1962), 26.
6   Guy E. Swanson, *Social Change* (Glenview, Ill, 1971), 166.
7   Cf Talcott Parsons, 'An Approach to Psychological Theory in Terms of the Theory of Action', in Sigmund Koch (ed), *Psychology: The Study of a Science*, vol 3 (New York, 1959), 614–19.
8   R. H. Tawney, *The Radical Tradition* (London, 1966), 89.
9   Ibid, 78.
10   Barrington Moore, *Social Origins of Dictatorship and Democracy* (London, 1966), ch VIII, 'Revolution from Above and Fascism'.
11   Cf E. J. Jones, *Some Aspects of Adult Education in Italy* (London, 1934).
12   Peter Calvert, *Revolution* (London, 1970), 109.
13   Ralph Waldo Emerson, 'Self Reliance', in *Essays, First and Second Series* (New York, nd), 33.
14   Chalmers Johnson, *Revolution and the Social System* (Stanford, 1964), 158.
15   Thomas Paine, *Rights of Man. Being an Answer to Mr Burke's Attack on the French Revolution* (London, 1930), 135.
16   This is Mazzini's comment on the French Revolution. Cf Guiseppe Mazzini, *The Duties of Man and other essays by Joseph Mazzini* (London, 1913), 251.
17   Reinhard Bendix, 'Social Stratification and Political Community', in Reinhard Bendix and Seymour Martin Lipset (eds): *Class Status and Power* (London, 1967), 84.
18   The concept of *veto-groups* is elaborated in David Riesman, *The Lonely Crowd* (New York, 1953), 257–8.
19   Richard Hoggart, *The Uses of Literacy* (London, 1969), 297.
20   The history of educational settlements in England is summarised in Thomas Kelly, *A History of Adult Education in Great Britain* (Liverpool, 1962), 261–3.
21   H. Fleming, *Education through Settlements* (Beechcroft Bulletin no 2, Birkenhead, 1922), 5.
22   Preoccupation in the inter-war years with problems of organisation and administration can be noted in contemporary issues of *The Tutor's Bulletin*, published by the Association of Tutorial Class Tutors. In August 1926, for example, the Bulletin is concerned with the questions, 'Should joint committees run one-year courses?' and with 'The Organisation of Tutorial Class Work in London'. The report in this issue of the 1926 Annual Conference at Easton Lodge shows that of the five sessions which were

held, four were concerned with topics which dealt with the administrative problems of holding one-year classes, organising the extra-mural department of a university, the appointment of tutors and the effectiveness of WEA organisation. The report of the fifth session on the 'Teaching of Psychology', shows how great was the concern with standards, and the relationship of the 'new psychology' to traditional liberal subjects.

23 Cohen, op cit, 171.
24 David Lockwood, 'Social Integration and System Integration', in George K. Zollschan and Walter Hirsh (eds), *Exploration in Social Change* (London, 1964), 244–56.
25 Cohen, op cit, 171.
26 A. K. C. Ottaway, *Education and Society* (London, 1953), 92.
27 Cf Keith Davis, *Human Relations at Work: The Dynamics of Organisational Behaviour* (New York, 1967), for an elaboration of the characteristics of this custodial model, one of the four models which he conceptualised as tools to explore further behaviour within organisations.
28 Cf Phillips Bradley, 'The University's Role in Workers' Education' in *Adult Education Journal*, vol 8, no 83 (April 1948), and *Report and Recommendation, Commission of Inquiry on the Workers' Educational Service of the University of Michigan* (Michigan Committee on Civil Rights, Detroit, 1949).
29 These terms are those used by A. John Allaway, *Thought and Action in Extra-Mural Work, Leicester, 1946–1966* (Leicester, 1967). The object of *reparative* courses is to introduce those who have never previously had the opportunity of courses of a university character. *Renovative* courses are aimed at helping the educationally and professionally qualified to familiarise themselves with new developments in their field of interest.
30 T. S. Eliot, *Essays Ancient and Modern* (London, 1949).
31 R. W. Livingstone, *Greek Ideas and Modern Life* (Oxford, 1935), 115.
32 Flann Campbell, 'Latin and the Elite Tradition in Education', in *The British Journal of Sociology*, vol XIX, no 3 (September 1968), 308–25.
33 Ibid, 313.

Part III

Counting the Cost: The Eighties

8

A University Adult Education Project with the Unemployed

KEVIN WARD

(Studies in Adult Education, 15, 1983.)

The scale of unemployment in the UK is well documented[1], and it is general knowledge that there was a mass increase in unemployment between 1979 and 1981 (when it doubled to 12%) when there was a large inflow of people on to the register and the duration of unemployment became longer. All groups in society are affected by unemployment today, but, according to the Manpower Services Commission, some groups are affected much more than others

> ... *the incidence of unemployment is uneven. Most workers are never unemployed ... white-collar workers and those in higher occupational groups are particularly favoured ... some groups are much more vulnerable than others*[2]

Moreover, the view that the current wave of unemployment is temporary can be seen as naive; unemployment will not simply disappear in the next possible upturn of the cycle; the growing workforce, declining employment in manufacturing industry and rationalisation (part of which is the impact of new technology) mean that unemployment is now structural.

This article gives an account of the initial stages of one adult education agency's response to the situation. There have been a variety of similar, small-scale initiatives throughout the country, each reflecting a different facet of related traditions within the British adult education service; there is the perception of the unemployed as a major 'disadvantaged' group and therefore worthy of positive discrimination, the tradition of working class education, and the concern for 'personally fulfilling' adult education. All the traditions are embedded firmly in the work of the Department of Adult and Continuing

Education at Leeds University which in spite of the middle-class bias of much of its work (in common with almost all other adult education agencies), has a history of working with 'socially and educationally' disadvantaged groups, and providing education for the working-class. The substantial industrial studies section of the Department's work has consisted exclusively of day-release and evening classes for trade unionists. In recent years, the Department has been successful in developing community adult education with local working-class groups in Leeds and Bradford.

Despite losing staff through public expenditure cuts in 1981/82, the Department was still keen to assess the contribution that could be made to working with educationally disadvantaged groups. Detailed discussions in the Department and the University resulted in the decision to establish a 'Pioneer Work' sector with Richard Taylor acting as co-ordinator and, in consultation with the HMI, to propose to the DES that a new full-time appointment be made to initiate, organise, teach and monitor a programme of work with the unemployed. Subsequently, following DES and University approval, Kevin Ward was appointed to this post in October 1982.[3]

A university adult education department should be well-equipped to conduct action-research in this field. A central concern of any university work should obviously be the research function. From the outset then, an important part of the project's work has been a careful monitoring and analysis of initiatives and courses. It is also important to stress that, although the project is initially developing a wide range of courses, some of them eventually may more appropriately be run by institutions other than a university adult education department.

Before the work with the unemployed formally started in October 1982, however, it was agreed that one person alone would be unable to initiate, organise, teach and monitor a sufficiently broad programme of work from which generalisations, or at least guidelines, could be drawn – especially given the short time-scale of a temporary post. After consultation with the HMI, therefore, a project team was established for work with the unemployed which involved a number of experienced part-time tutors, in addition to K. Ward and R. Taylor.

Overall, £30,000 was made available for this work in 1982/83. This covers the costs of four part-time tutors working seven hours per week in Leeds and Bradford; it also pays for specialist tutors for specific short courses. By the end of 1982 then, the Department was making a much more significant contribution to adult education with the unemployed than it had done previously. The main problem with this finance, however, is that it is only guaranteed for one year. At the time of writing (March 1983) attempts are being made to secure further funding from the DES, but the financial future of the project – after only six months work – is, in common with many other 'unemployed initiatives', extremely precarious. This financial uncertainty has a detrimental impact on staff morale and forward planning, and makes it increasingly difficult for the project to retain legitimacy with a wide-range of organisations and groups.

There are two main objectives for this work which clearly fit into the DES liberal tradition of adult education. First, to provide opportunities for unemployed adults to pursue and develop a wide range of liberal studies, which may provide important sources of personal satisfaction and help to restore some of the self-confidence and self-esteem which have almost invariably been damaged by the stigma of unemployment. And second, to provide opportunities within the social studies area for unemployed people to gain a clearer understanding, both individually and collectively, of their situation and the ways in which it might be improved.

It was decided to develop a broad-based and varied pattern of provision in order to pursue these objectives. This was possible because the project-team (as distinct from two individuals) enabled different approaches to educational work with the unemployed to be developed and monitored. Nor are the unemployed a homogeneous group. Unemployment is experienced differently for example, by school-leavers who have never had jobs before, skilled and semi-skilled workers from manufacturing industries who are made redundant, and women who may have had intermittent histories of part-time working. Given these obvious differences, it seemed important to develop a variety of approaches each to be monitored on a separate basis.

(i) *Organisational:* i.e. working in close co-operation with organisations specifically concerned with the unemployed. These include TUC Centres for the Unemployed, Drop-in Centres and other 'out-of-work' centres.

(ii) *Trade Union oriented:* i.e. the development of contacts both at different levels within trade unions (e.g. full-time officials, shop-stewards, branch-members) and also between trade unions, to explore the feasibility of educational provision for unemployed members.

(iii) *Community oriented:* i.e. the development of a network of contacts through community groups, small voluntary bodies, tenants' associations and neighbourhood groups.

(iv) *Institutional:* i.e. working with other educational and related bodies, e.g. LEA, WEA, to facilitate not only direct provision but the flow of information and the creation of a wide-ranging counselling system.

Before outlining some of the issues which have arisen in the first few months of the project's existence, it is necessary to refer to a number of characteristics which should be present in educational work with the unemployed, whatever approach is being adopted. Initially at least, the education which is being offered should be on a non-formal basis, and the content of learning should be closely related to both the environment and the recognised needs of the learners. As Saul Alinsky put it: 'the first requirement for education is for people to have a reason for knowing'.[4] Secondly, it has to be recognised that most of the unemployed are working-class people living in relative poverty, and that education must help them in this situation. This, in practical terms, means providing the information and the knowledge-base with which the unemployed can deal with their welfare-rights problems. Another characteristic of non-formal education is that there should be no formal qualifications for admission, no restrictions on participation, and provision must be free – this is essential, given the close link that exists between poverty and unemployment.[5] There should then be an emphasis initially on the learning of specific, useful knowledge which is recognised as such by the participants and on the development of attitudes which may lead to increased self-confidence.

These then should be essential starting points in developing adult education with the unemployed: they obviously involve a breakdown of traditional hierarchical assumptions about 'teacher' and 'student'. It was decided by the full-time and part-time workers on the project that these same principles should apply to the workings of the project team. A co-operative, non-hierarchical structure has been devised which involves a critical sharing of experiences, and decisions being taken on a team basis. This aspect of the project's work obviously leads to more meetings for all concerned, but the trust and the support which this structure has engendered means that all the workers are committed to it.

After four months, sixty-two courses for the unemployed had been organised in Leeds and Bradford. Most of this provision has been in the form of short courses lasting eight weeks. The project provided tutors and all the courses were free. The broad subject-areas and the details of the syllabus were jointly worked out between tutors and the unemployed 'students'. A broad spread of chosen areas may be categorised as follows:

(a) *'Survival' courses:* Welfare-rights are the prime example in this category and seventeen 'Know Your Rights' courses have been organised. Given the close link between unemployment and poverty, it is not surprising that these courses have been popular. The unemployed certainly have a strong reason for wanting to know about these issues. It is, then, relevant learning which is closely related to their environment and their (expressed) needs. These courses do not attempt to 'train' people to become 'experts'; rather they provide a broad introduction which is practical – because it is based on students' own experiences and needs – but which is also directly 'educational' because tutors locate these practicalities in a particular socio-economic context and attempt to develop discussion round a number of social policy issues. Another 'survival' course is 'You and the Police' which is currently being organised in the predominantly black Chapeltown area of Leeds. This course also provides an educational opportunity to give information on, to analyse and to discuss a number of directly relevant issues.

(b) *Discussion Groups:* Twelve informal discussion groups have been organised. These have sometimes emerged alongside other 'courses', but they have also developed where a group of people wish to meet, but not with the discussion of any specific subject-area in mind. These groups have been valuable in discussing issues surrounding unemployment: individual experiences again can be located in a broader context. They have also helped to overcome the personal pathology – or individual blame – model of unemployment and can restore at least some self-confidence and self-esteem.

(c) *'New Opportunities' courses:* These have sometimes developed after welfare-rights courses. Individuals often want to know what opportunities and possibilities are open to them. It has proved useful to discuss these possible options in groups as well as to provide some individual educational counselling because the group context can, as in all other courses, build up an individual's self-confidence. Again, it is not simply a case of providing information: this is done but it is critically evaluated. For example, information (which has already been acted upon by several unemployed people) about mature entry to university is located within the context of the middle-class bias of the higher education system. These sessions have examined possibilities for entry into full or part-time educational courses where people are interested in gaining qualifications or aiming for a 'career'; other options and possible interests of the group can be examined, whether this be education for leisure or interest, education about community or political activity, or a critical examination of 'training' possibilities, whether through skills-centres or MSC programmes.

It is important to stress that in both the discussion-groups and in the new opportunities courses, there is detailed political, psychological and sociological discussion resulting from the tutors' contributions and the students' personal experiences. The rationale for these courses then is fundamentally educational.

(d) *Subject-Area Courses:* a wide range of traditional and not-so-traditional courses have been organised. These include economics, psychology, drama, politics and contemporary Rock music. There are clearly a number of reasons why people choose these courses; they include political interest, personal-recreational motives, using these courses as 'tasters' for longer courses or returning to study. In fact, there are already a number of students who, after detailed discussions with tutors, have applied for full-time courses as mature students. These include entry into university courses and adult college courses.

These then are the categories of courses which have recently been developed. In practice, there is often an overlap between these different categories, and courses for some groups or organisations may include elements of all four categories.

The courses described above have been used in a variety of contexts. These different settings for the development of educational work with the unemployed must now be examined.

Organisations for the Unemployed

Given that one prerequisite for the project was to make contact with unemployed groups and individuals, it was clearly vital to establish close liaison and co-ordination with those organisations already working with the unemployed. In Leeds and Bradford this has meant working closely with the TUC Centres for the Unemployed[6] and an independent organisation of the unemployed called TOWCAS (The Out of Work Centre and Advisory Service). The project helped to organise educational open-days for these organisations, and from these, a number of courses subsequently developed. These included welfare-rights (the most common subject), politics, music, drama, psychology, economics and discussion groups. In all, twenty-six classes (approximately 42% of total provision) have so far been organised for and with Organisations for the Unemployed.

In practice, it was only possible to organise these courses because individuals from the project had established legitimacy and close working relationships with staff and volunteers at these centres, long before the project officially started.

To a large extent, of course the project was dependent on these organisations working effectively in attracting unemployed people. It was no accident in Leeds that initially six courses were successfully organised with TOWCAS but only two at the Centre for the Unemployed. At that time, TOWCAS had been in existence nearly two years and the unemployed volunteers running the organisation were well-established. The Centre for the Unemployed, however, which had just recently been opened, was struggling to develop both its identity and its clientele. It experienced many problems: located in the city centre, but without, at that time, the membership organisation which TOWCAS had; factional struggles in the local Trades Council about the control of the Management Committee; TUC/MSC guidelines to follow; internal conflicts between inexperienced MSC workers – and all of these problems were present even before detailed contacts with unemployed people could be made, and priorities established between campaigning, educational and recreational activities.

Those of us working on the adult education project could not resolve these problems for the Centre – that was primarily the task of the Centre's management committee and workers. We provided informal support, but it was essential for us not to rely exclusively on reaching unemployed people through organisations like TOWCAS and the Centre for the Unemployed. We felt that it was crucial to work with these organisations but we also needed to develop broad-based and varied approaches to this work.

Therefore, in addition to working with organisations for the unemployed, we have also been developing a trade union, a community and an institutional approach to work with the unemployed. These approaches are all in early stages of development but it is still possible to outline a number of relevant points.

Trade Union Work

In 1982, the TUC General Council stated: 'Unions must find ways of involving and helping the jobless', and urged members to develop a nationwide programme of discussions and meetings about unemployment. These statements reflect obvious genuine concern for the unemployed by many people at different levels within the Trade Union Movement. The TUC could argue that their action in establishing the 180 Centres for the Unemployed (albeit only possible because of approximately £3 million from the MSC) proves that they want to take practical measures for the unemployed as well as pass resolutions about the issue.

The fact remains however that not one single trade union has as yet developed any systematic programme 'for involving and helping the jobless.' The gap between the employed and the unemployed remains as wide as ever. Several quotations from a recent survey[7] illustrate this point:

> ... (there is) a feeling by many of the unemployed that they have been betrayed, ignored or rejected by trade unionists and their organi-

> *sations . . . (unemployed) people see unions as the ones who let them go*
> *down the road . . . many of the unemployed do not consider the trade*
> *union movement very supportive.*

Apart from any moral concern for the unemployed, it is obviously in the political interests of individual unions to attempt to bridge this enormous gap between those in, and those out of work.

We therefore decided to approach one major Leeds Trade Union which had experienced large job-losses, in order to see whether it was possible to create interest in at least initiating educational work for and with their unemployed members.

The engineering industry has suffered particularly throughout the recession in recent years, as manufacturing generally has declined. In Leeds, for example, between 1974–1980, at least 12,000 jobs have been lost from such firms as Rank Optics, Greenbat Epco, and Crabtree Vickers which were formerly at the heart of the city's manufacturing industry.[8] Since 1979 there has been a further steep decline in engineering and consequently much higher rates of job loss. For example, metal manufacturing nationally lost 26% of its jobs between 1979–1981.[9] In the same period, the mechanical, electrical and instrument sectors of the engineering industry lost 350,000 jobs.[10]

Given these facts, we approached the AUEW District Committee in Leeds in an attempt, first, to create practical – as distinct from rhetorical – interest in the plight of their unemployed members. If we were successful in this, then we could suggest developing an educational programme for and with their unemployed members: this to be controlled by the Union but jointly organised by the project and the Union. It is important to outline the process which was followed in this work. First we had informal discussions with a number of experienced shop stewards; then we had formal meetings with the district committee. Subsequently we developed detailed proposals with a sub-committee from the district on educational work with the unemployed. This stage of the work lasted more than three months and illustrates one obvious general point about developing educational work with and through individual unions. Working through official union structures and committee cycles is an essential but slow process. One certainly cannot expect any short-term results from it.

Eventually, after lengthy discussions, publicity was produced and distributed to all branches and shop steward committees about a weekly course which was to start in AEU House (the union's district headquarters) for unemployed members. Since (at the time of writing) this 'course' has been in existence less than two months, it is difficult to generalise about it, but already some preliminary comments can be made.

Even though the course consists only of twelve unemployed engineers, it is the first such initiative in the country that AUEW have officially developed. Indeed it is difficult to find many examples of other individual unions organising such work.

The first stages of the course have provided introductory sessions on
1. Welfare Rights,
2. General discussion on experiences and causes of unemployment,
3. New Opportunities.

The group has rapidly become very enthusiastic so that even at this early stage they intend to produce a pack of information, based on the course, which can be used by all their unemployed members. For the first time, albeit on a very modest level, there has been contact between employed and unemployed members; the group has successfully persuaded the district committee to subsidise bus fares for all who attend the course, and to produce further publicity. The district committee also receives regular progress reports.

There are already a number of spin-offs from this development. The Leeds Branch of TASS invited speakers from the project and are now encouraging their unemployed members to attend the same sessions. Informal meetings have also taken place with other unions and, if the project had guaranteed resources (which it has not), then it would be possible to develop similar programmes with them.

Whatever happens in the future, certain lessons have already been learnt. First, there is a need for detailed contact-work and discussion to take place long before any specific 'courses' are planned or contact made with the unemployed: this process provides the basis for partnership and co-operation so that resources can be co-ordinated and maximised. In this case, this meant practically that the project provided tutors for the course and the union paid for publicity, administration etc. Secondly, in line with the characteristics of non-formal education, when courses are publicised they must include relevant information for working-class people – this point obviously applies to all the approaches which are being developed.

The Community Approach

In addition to working with and through organisations for the unemployed and trade unions, it was also decided to develop a selective community approach. By working with and through local community groups (tenants' groups local community-centre management committees etc) and sympathetic adult education centres, the project was able to develop eighteen courses in the first four months.

These included several alternative health courses in Bradford which were attended mainly by women. Eight Welfare Rights courses were organised and again, several of these were attended mainly by women. Bearing in mind that the unemployed are not a homogeneous group, and that many women in particular neither see themselves as unemployed, nor are they included in official unemployment statistics, it was decided deliberately to organise some courses which were not explicitly aimed at the unemployed. Because all the courses (except one) were held during the day, they attracted some women who were in fact unemployed but would not have attended something specifically for the unemployed.

In addition to Health and Welfare Rights, courses were also organised on Housing Rights, New Ways to Work, You and the Police, plus general drop-in and discussion groups. As mentioned above, all (except one) of these were day-time courses and provided free of charge. The location and publicity for these courses varied according to local circumstances. One drop-in discussion group and the New Ways to Work course met in a well-known and accessible adult education centre. Local publicity was extensive, with the use of posters and leaflets. In contrast to this, one of the Welfare Rights courses was held in a council house on a large estate and attended entirely by people from neighbouring streets. Publicity for this was done purely by word of mouth. An active member of the tenants' association in that area felt that the local community centre was too far away and that people would more willingly come to a friend's house. This arrangement however was only possible because the project had close contact with members of the local groups.

It should be clear from these brief illustrations that in adopting a 'community approach', detailed knowledge of and contact with a wide variety of local groups is a prerequisite. The courses referred to above were able to be organised in the first few months of the project's existence, only because the workers already had detailed knowledge of and close contacts with local groups and organisations.

An Institutional Approach

This fourth and final approach to work with the unemployed which the project is developing involves working with other educational related bodies to facilitate, not only direct provision, but the flow of information and the development of a wide-ranging counselling system. These various approaches which are being outlined are clearly not watertight compartments. Thus, in practice, this institutional approach overlaps with the community approach as the project has developed joint work with the LEA and the WEA. One example of this approach was the development of a mental health group by the project and the WEA. The project provided a tutor-organiser who liaised closely with the WEA Mental Health Worker. They drew together a group of people who were leaving various day-centres or psychiatric institutions, and the project worker organised a weekly current affairs discussion group. This group has now been meeting successfully for several months, and as a result of this, five members of the group – who would certainly not even have considered the possibility previously – have now become members of TOWCAS (the independent organisation of the unemployed in Leeds which was referred to earlier) and joined courses there. This is just one small example of creating links between various groups who are affected by unemployment – but it is only possible when several agencies work closely together.

On a more general note, this institutional approach clearly involves close co-operation with other agencies. In Leeds and Bradford collaborative arrangements have been developed with the LEAs in a number of ways: the project has been given free use of all premises and liaises closely with city-centre local authority provision such as a Drop-in Educational and Advice Centre. In Bradford, the project has worked particularly closely with the local authority in servicing a Local Development Council for Adult Education, and a Forum (consisting of both agencies and unemployed people) which is a focal point for discussion and action on education initiatives with the unemployed. In this way, a broad spectrum of 'courses' and opportunities for the unemployed can be developed from basic literacy and maths, through either to the range of special courses which the project can offer, or to what would traditionally be referred to as non-vocational liberal adult education. This cooperation obviously avoids the danger of duplication and when resources are as scarce as they are in adult education, then this alone is an important factor.

Conclusion

The Leeds Project then is in the early stages of learning a number of lessons about organising educational work with the unemployed through the four approaches which have been outlined above.

Even at this early stage it is plain that the provision of sixty-two courses for the unemployed involving more than seven hundred students, in the first few months of the project's existence, clearly demonstrates that there is a demand, and indeed an urgent need, for 'non-vocational' adult education courses with various groups of unemployed adults. However, it is only possible to develop this work by carefully and systematically adhering to some of the characteristics of non-formal education. For example, the need for 'relevant' education which is closely related to the environment of participants is clearly illustrated by the fact that more than one-quarter of the 'courses' were in the Welfare-Rights area. Most of the unemployed are working-class living in absolute or relative poverty and dependent on state-benefits: any educational providers then, must be aware of the implications of this.

One issue which is particularly significant for university adult education is the counselling, organisational and co-ordinatory roles which tutors must develop in addition to their teaching roles. The description of the four approaches adopted by the project clearly shows that they all require significant counselling and developmental work, before and during any courses which are provided. With the trade union approach, two tutors spent three months on preparatory work before a course was even advertised. This expanded role of a university adult education tutor is particularly difficult for part-time tutors with limited paid hours, but is absolutely essential if work with the unemployed, and indeed working-class education generally, is to be developed.

Not only is it necessary to expand the role of the adult educator for this type of work: it is also important to reassess critically traditional adult education teaching. The tutor is not simply a pedagogue or the expert in some specialist subject; rather

> *through dialogue, the teacher-of-the-students and the students-of-the-teacher cease to exist and a new term emerges: teacher-student with student-teachers. The teacher is no longer merely the one-who-teaches, but is himself taught in dialogue with the students, who in turn, while being taught, also teach. They become jointly responsible for a process in which all grow.[11]*

There are important implications here for the roles and possible changing status positions of adult educators from a variety of settings. Attempts must be made to allow groups to control the learning situation itself and its underlying aims: the tutors must be as accountable to these groups as they are to their employing bodies. This joint responsibility has already been apparent in the project's work. The unemployed engineers group wishes to continue Welfare-Rights courses and discussion on a range of issues related to unemployment: the project's tutors provide input for this. In addition however, the group is also developing ideas about bridging the gap between the employed and the unemployed in their particular union and establishing mechanisms for this. The group then has decided that it wishes both to have education which is relevant to the needs of its members and to work politically within their union over the general issue of unemployment.

In other contexts, groups may wish to study particular subjects for leisure and/or as an introduction to longer courses, perhaps involving access to higher education. It is crucially important then, both for the immediate course details and also the underlying aims and implications of the educational process to be jointly discussed and decided upon by tutors and students.

It was stated earlier in this article that there are no major current or planned initiatives to meet the educational and training needs of the adult unemployed. Whatever the shortcomings of the Youth Training Scheme, at least the issues of youth unemployment, training, and somewhat belatedly, the relationship between education and training, are being discussed. With the adult unemployed, there is no such provision or discussion although the recently published *New Training Initiative* (MSC) does consider the needs of the adult. It is all the more urgent therefore for adult education agencies, whether they be LEAs, the WEA, or university adult education departments to develop such discussions. It is very important however that these be based on guidelines which have been established through giving priority (both in policy and in practice) to developing work with the unemployed as part of a move away from the persistent middle-class bias of current adult education provision.

References

1   For official statistics, cf *Department of Employment Gazette*, published monthly; for details of recent changes in the way unemployment statistics are gathered, cf *Employment Gazette* September 1982 and IDS *Report 387*, October 1982. For critiques of official figures cf *Education for unemployed adults*, ACACE, December 1982, Appendix A; *Labour Research*, December 1982 and April, 1983; *Unemployment, the fight for TUC alternatives*, TUC, 1981; *Unemployment, studies for trade unionists*, Vol 8 No 30, WEA, 1982; *Unemployment: who pays the price?* Ed L. Burghes and R. Lister, CPAG Poverty Pamphlet No 53, 1981; cf also, *The workless state*, B. Showler and A. Sinfield, Martin Robertson, 1981; and *What unemployment means*, A. Sinfield, Martin Robertson, 1981.

2   *MSC Manpower Review*, London MSC, 1980, p 13.

3   In common with other similar projects, funding was only made available for an appointment for two to three years on a 'pilot' basis.

4   S. Alinsky, *Rules for radicals*, Vintage Books, 1972.

5   For evidence on this, cf 'Unemployment and Poverty'. L. Burghes, Ch 5 in *Unemployment: who pays the price?*, op cit.

6   For further information on the TUC Centres for the Unemployed, cf *Labour Research* February 1983.

7   *Labour Research*, op cit.

8   *The economic and social crisis in west Yorkshire*. Leeds TUCRIC, 1981.

9   *New Society*, 10 September 1981.

10 *TUC/Economic Review*, 1982, Ch 1.

11 P. Freire, *Pedagogy of the Oppressed*, Penguin, 1972.

9

Conformity and Contradiction in English Responsible Body Adult Education, 1925–1950

ROGER FIELDHOUSE
(Studies in the Education of Adults, 17, 1985.)

> *To ensure stability, societies set limits on the kinds of behaviour which are tolerable, and arrange a set of sanctions for those who break those limits. The boundaries set are arbitrary . . .*
> J. E. Thomas, *Radical Adult Education: Theory and Practice* (1982), p13.

This article[1] will attempt to define and delineate the ideological boundaries of English Responsible Body (RB) adult education during the second quarter of the twentieth century, which encompassed the broad centre of the British political spectrum, accommodating notions of individual fulfilment, social purpose, public service, social justice and class emancipation, and sometimes bordering on the subversive, but ultimately conforming to a rationalist and reformist consensus which kept more 'extreme' influences at bay.

The Oxford reform movement at the beginning of the twentieth century was very influential in the formulation of this radical-liberal ideology. The Oxford (and particularly Balliol) social conscience and commitment to social reform and a life of action gave rise to a circumscribed or cautious radicalism which could be found in varying degrees in the political ideas of such colossi of the English adult education movement as William Temple, R.H. Tawney, A.D. Lindsay and G.D.H. Cole.[2] Although they were at times intellectually critical of the labour movement, they gave it a vast amount of support. And although at times they (or at least Tawney and Cole) came close to a quasi-Marxist or revolutionary perspective, they all rejected the authoritarianism of Leninist-

Stalinism and the more elitist aspects of Fabian 'police collectivism'. Despite some flirtations (particularly by Cole) with 'direct democracy', they remained faithful to the rationalist and reformist parliamentary road to socialism and to the bourgeois notion of representative democracy. Ultimately they rejected the thesis that within a capitalist society there was an inherent and inevitable antagonistic relationship of classes which could only be resolved by class war. They occupied a position in the political spectrum which ranged between the social-democratic, reformist centre and the 'non-Marxist ethical socialism of the Labour left'.[3] This represented the ideological mainstream of English adult education which had such close links with the labour movement that at times adult education and labour seemed to be part and parcel of the same movement.

These close links were personified by innumerable tutors, administrators, and students who were active in the labour movement,[4] to the extent that the Board of Education noted somewhat caustically of the Workers' Educational Association (WEA) in 1925 that:

> *... while it may be said that the teachers are not serving the ends of political parties, the membership of the classes in certain areas is recruited in ways (e.g. through the Trade Unions) which make it inevitable that the students belong in the main, if not exclusively, to one political party ... If one regards the political opinions of the active members of the Committees of the Association it might almost be said that the Association has very close relations with the Labour Party.*[5]

After the Second World War, the newly-elected Labour government and Labour-dominated House of Commons included many who attributed their education to, or were closely associated with, the adult education movement. These included a WEA Vice-President, Arthur Creech Jones, who was Under Secretary, and later Secretary of State, for the Colonies; fourteen other members of the Goverment, including the Chancellor of the Exchequer; and many Labour back-benchers who were tutors, former tutors or members of the WEA executive.[6] And for many years before that, the WEA had campaigned very zealously for educational reforms and other political actions which were similar to, if not identical with, Labour Party policy, and, particularly through Tawney, had helped to formulate the Labour Party's policies.[7] The predominantly labourist attitudes of many tutors and students, and their syllabuses and favourite text books, have been described in an earlier article.[8]

In contrast (despite occasional complaints about subversive activities) there was widespread antipathy to, or ignorance of, Marxist ideas[9] and equally little sympathy with conservative political philosophy. Conservatives complained to the Board of Education that they were made to feel unwelcome by the adult education bodies.[10] It is difficult to find any evidence of active, committed Conservatives who were adult education tutors. Two of the few exceptions, Frank Pakenham and his future wife, Elizabeth Harman, were soon converted to socialism and became active members of the Labour Party.[11]

There were other Conservatives who taught adult education classes, such as R. Bassett, an Oxford staff tutor with markedly pro-Chamberlain views, and Arthur Bryant, the 'well-known Conservative' who was in fact an officer of the Conservative College at Ashridge Park,[12] but they were few and far between. Indeed, an article by Bryant in *The Highway* in late 1937, outlining his Conservative views, caused a major controversy in the WEA's journal. The editor had to defend the WEA's obligation to 'give a Conservative like Bryant as ready a hearing as Attlee or Pollitt' against accusations that Bryant's views were suitable for the capitalist press, but not *The Highway*.[13] The Vice-Chairman of the Yorkshire North WEA District spelled out the working class basis of the Association and argued that this required a closer connection with the labour movement than with the Conservative Party. This meant selecting tutors who were in sympathy with 'our movement' – not going out of the way 'to invite people with whom we have nothing in common, whose aims are not ours . . . Nor can it mean that we shall use the same efforts to get hold of groups of the conservative party as we shall to get hold of groups of labour political people . . . it cannot mean either that we shall welcome men like Bryant as tutors as readily as we shall men like Crossman.'[14] This perhaps contradicted the sentiments of many of the 600 correspondents who wrote in support of *The Highway's* publication of Bryant's article, but it confirmed the complaint of one of those correspondents that 'the WEA habitually renders uncomfortable the position of persons holding Conservative or Right Wing views who participate in its movement. Its' "impartiality" extends no further than a contemptuous toleration of Liberalism.'[15]

Thus both the class analysis of the left and the absolutism and paternalism of the right were banished beyond the pale of adult education, which was broadly liberal, sometimes radical, sometimes pluralist, but essentially anti-Marxist and anti-conservative in its overall tenor.

Of course the adult education movement attracted some right wing and even more communist and Marxist tutors[16] but in the popular front atmosphere of the 1930s and the progressive unity of the immediate post-war period, this was not generally seen as a challenge to the bourgeois-liberal hegemony. Until the cold war polarised politics in the late 1940s, the occasional Marxist was not regarded as a threat to the predominantly labourist ideology of the adult education movement. Its comfortably affinity with the British liberal tradition seemed to offer a welcome alternative to the revolutionary perspective of the

Communist Party and the National Council of Labour Colleges (NCLC) – the perceived real enemies of the state. For all its occasional lapses, the adult education movement was welcomed by the establishment as a bulwark against revolutionism, a moderating influence and a form of social control. It helped to channel and reduce pressures and conflict, neutralise class antagonism and integrate the working class into British society – just like its 'partner', the Labour Party.

This was recognised by Lord Eustace Percy, the Conservative President of the Board of Education, when he noted in 1925:

> *In adult education there is a continual struggle going on between the Universities and those bodies, like the Workers' Educational Association, who work with the Universities, on the one hand, and the Communist or semi-Communist Labour Colleges on the other. Hitherto the Workers' Educational Association and the University Extension people have been able to make headway against these undesirable propagandists because, largely owing to Government assistance, they can offer better facilities. On the whole, too, I think the education that they do offer is extraordinarily useful ... If we force the WEA and the Universities to cut down their work we shall not choke off the demand for local classes which is extraordinarily strong in all parts of the country, but we shall open a wide door to the Labour Colleges, and I believe that the result will be deplorable. In fact my own view is that £100,000 spent annually on this kind of work, properly controlled, would be about the best police expenditure we could indulge in ...* [17]

It was thus because of its affinity with, but ultimate rejection of, the politics of the revolutionary 'left' that the adult education movement was so valuable to the establishment. It attracted potential working class activists and leaders by its radical image, but diverted them from the communist or revolutionary politics to which they might otherwise have been drawn. There were therefore two political reasons for the state funding of RB adult education, to promote and maintain a very typically British political safety-valve, and to control its head of steam.

Although many individuals were unaware of or unaffected by any state controls, there is no doubt that on occasions the powers enjoyed by central government and the LEAs to grant or withhold essential financial aid provided them with a means of policing and controlling the adult education movement. One such occasion occurred when both central and local government threatened to withdraw grant aid to the WEA in 1925 because it was felt that its participation in the proposed TUC education scheme undermined adult education's valuable neutralising role, as envisaged by Lord Eustace Percy, by bringing it too much under the influence of the trade union movement, the Labour Party and (most seriously) the Marxist NCLC.[18] The authorities therefore sought assurances about the WEA's good behaviour and imposed certain conditions for grant, including a very restrictive interpretation of the TUC scheme, the abandonment of adult education's traditional specific identification with the working class, and a stricter interpretation of the WEA's non-party-political status. They also insisted that classes should be open to LEA inspection and approval, and sought means by which the LEAs could keep the WEA 'carefully scrutinised' or replace it altogether 'where the work of the WEA becomes unsatisfactory'.[19] Although the TUC scheme was never implemented, the affair demonstrated how grant aid was used to impose more effective machinery for supervision and control, and to prevent the RBs from stepping outside their bounds.

During the subsequent two decades, there was little evidence of heavy censorship or control, but there were a number of controversial or suspicious incidents which were investigated. For example, the HMIs were unhappy about what they perceived as an undue concentration on political and social topics in literature and history adult education classes in Yorkshire, Lancashire and Cheshire during 1927–28, which offered lessons of a rather different kind to the national issues they had in mind.[20]

In 1930, the local education committee, the local MP and the local HMI all undertook investigations into the WEA's activities in Torquay when there was an alleged 'deliberate attempt to bring in a side issue of politics . . . [and] make the WEA part of the Labour Movement in Torquay.'[21] Three years later, Ernest Green, the WEA General Secretary, had to give an undertaking to the Parliamentary Secretary to the President of the Board of Education that the WEA would avoid political improprieties after the Conservative Party South-Eastern Area Agents' Association and several local Conservative MPs accused the WEA Medway Towns Branch and one of its tutors, H. L. Beales, of socialistic or communist propagandising.[22] About this same time, the Director of Education for West Sussex made several complaints to the local WEA District Secretary, J.H. Matthews, concerning the bohemian life style and left-wing associates of J.R. Armstrong, who worked both for the WEA Southern District and Southampton University College extramural department.[23]

HMIs admonished a Liverpool staff tutor for being 'very much in the labour interest',[24] and classes provided by Hull University College and Birmingham University in 1933–34 were criticised for their alleged political bias and tolerance of the unpatriotic views of students.[25] The general feeling expressed in the reports was that there was altogether too much intemperate, pejorative and injudicious bias being permitted if not encouraged by the tutors. Some years later, HMI Dann expressed similar criticisms about the 'intemperance' of R.H.S. Crossman and G.D.H. Cole because they identified the interests of adult education too closely with those of the working class.[26] A year later Cole was again a subject of complaint when he was described by the South Berkshire Conservative Association Agent, C.F.R. Bagnall, as 'a well known local socialist.'[27] Bagnall complained to the local Conservative MP that Cole chaired a WEA Meeting at Thatcham where a 'Mr. Jardine of Andover ... [gave] a tub-thumping speech ... on Communism and the Russian system ... and the usual left wing claptrap [was] produced.'[28]

In the North Staffs WEA District before the war there was a constant stream of complaints to the District Secretary, George Wigg, about the political activities of his tutors,[29] while in the Cambridge area HMI Jack believed there were a few WEA tutors 'who did not too clearly distinguish between academic teaching and propaganda.'[30] Jack was also critical of the political commitment sometimes shown by a Cambridge extramural tutor, John Hampden Jackson. He was also involved in the investigations into another Cambridge tutor, Maurice Bruce, whose reference to the 1919 Amritsar massacre as a decisive factor in changing Gandhi's attitude to the British administration in India at a class at Wellingborough in 1939 was mis-reported in the local paper and caused the local Conservative MP, Wing Commander A.W.H. James, to suspect Bruce of raising trouble about the government's Indian policy.[31] James asked the Board of Education to obtain a satisfactory explanation, threatening otherwise to raise the matter in the House of Commons. Jack was dispatched to Cambridge to question Geoffrey Hickson, Secretary of the Cambridge Board of Extramural Studies, about Bruce, and to examine Bruce closely about his views.[32]

These investigations established a code of conduct – always with the explicit or implicit threat that failure to comply with the code would result in withdrawal of grant aid. In this way the RBs were persuaded to loosen their close ties with the working class and the labour movement and to pay less attention to specifically working class interests. They were encouraged to see themselves as broader adult education providers for all sectors of society. They were warned against 'intemperate' left wing bias or over-concern with mere social and working conditions instead of larger (more worthy) national issues.

The outbreak of war not unnaturally increased the political pressures and brought much closer to the surface the conflict that always existed between what tutors might conceive of as objective scholarship and what the establishment paymasters might consider to be the national interest. In the early months of 1940, HMIs Jack and Dann submitted reports to the Board of Education on the problem of controversial topics in adult education. They were anxious for the Board to realise the inflammable nature of many of the topics dealt with in adult education, including 'international relations, causes of war, the character of the peace, federal union and so forth'.[33] 'Such topics if indiscreetly handled either by accident or design on the part of the lecturer might easily give rise to a storm of protest accompanied by questions in the House which the Board would find extremely embarrassing' warned a Board official in a minute paper circulated internally in May 1940.[34] It was also noted that the Board had received 'various letters from individuals complaining of certain tutors in this connection. We have *mostly* been able to satisfy ourselves that in these cases the complaints could be answered' but it was necessary to realise that 'the temper of people is easily roused at present and with the increase of casualties and danger may become more readily roused still'.[35] This was a clear warning that the adult education movement should be even more careful not no stray beyond the permissible boundaries.

The Board of Education was especially worried about indiscretions arising from 'the left wing character of so many of the lecturers and their disciples'.[36] It was not considered feasible to prohibit classes in these controversial subjects, given the lively interest in them at this time, but the Board did consider issuing a circular 'stressing the necessity of treating such topics objectively and impartially and of avoiding any ground for complaint that the Board are encouraging an anti-national point of view' (thus identifying objectivity and impartiality with the national point of view).[37] It was also to be intimated 'that any lapse from propriety would jeopardise payment of grant.'[38] However, the fear of appearing over-censorious deterred the Board from issuing its circular: instead it persuaded the Central Joint Advisory Committee on Tutorial Classes (representing the RBs) to issue its own statement on 'The Handling of Controversial Subjects in War-time' which exhorted tutors to show a patriotic objectivity and a sense of responsibility which paid due deference to what the establishment defined as the national interest.[39]

War-time nervousness, and the growth of informal adult education which was increasingly popular in the WEA and many extramural departments, did give rise to a number of controversial incidents and official warnings,[40] but it was in the civilian contribution to education for HM Forces that the RBs experienced more direct control by the authorities because of the fears about security and the difference between the Services' and the RBs' perceptions of education. The Services were dubious about, or even hostile to, free discussion of controversial subjects. They regarded education as an adjunct to military training or as an antidote to boredom at times of enforced idleness. The military demand for unquestioning obedience was in direct conflict with adult education's Socratic approach. The established procedures for dealing with lectures or incidents about which the Services felt concerned did sometimes inhibit free discussion of topics which were normally considered the very heart of adult education. And the security vetting (and the Services' ultimate veto) in the appointment of lecturers amounted to a political filter. Various categories of tutors who were not acceptable to the Services – pacifists, aliens, conscientious objectors and all those who expressed views which the military authorities (or MI5) considered subversive (either because they were critical of war policy or threatened to 'undermine the fabric of society') – were liable to be debarred from this aspect of the RB's work. Although the number of bannings during the war was relatively small, it was sufficient to induce a wariness and caution amongst the approved tutors when dealing with political and controversial subjects. This was exactly what was intended. It created a pressure to conform.[41]

After the war, the spread of cold war attitudes soon affected adult education, imposing upon it a much narrower definition of acceptability and a much restricted consensus. This caused controversies and constraints, especially in the growing field of trade union education. It was seriously questioned whether Marxists or communists should be allowed to teach in adult education, and a certain amount of witch hunting occurred in various extramural departments, including Birmingham, Leeds, Liverpool, London, Manchester and Oxford.[42] At Oxford, the suspicions and accusations of the WEA General Secretary led to enquiries into the 1948 Queen's College trade union school and into trade union courses at the Wedgwood Memorial College. Although nothing untoward was discovered about the Queen's school, attempts were made to prevent communist tutors taking part the next year. At the Wedgwood Memorial College the investigation did consider that some tutors had shown an indiscreet warmth towards communism and that the Warden had committed an error of judgment in employing a disproportionately large number of communists or 'fellow-travellers' as tutors. It was felt that this offended against the cold war political consensus and alienated the trade union hierarchy. The contracts of the Warden and one other left wing tutor were not renewed and there was a general reduction of Marxist influence. After this, a more social-democratic range of values prevailed at Oxford under the guardianship of the new Secretary of the Tutorial Classes Committee, Frank Pickstock.

Whilst the McCarthyism at Oxford was not imposed directly by the State, the extramural department's dependence on public funding made it susceptible to the pressures of the cold war political climate. This was equally, if not more, true of the WEA, which became very sensitive to accusations of subversion, and over-anxious to prove itself innocent of such charges. Complaints about the WEA's alleged left wing bias led to action being taken against those who, in the cold war climate, were deemed to have shown too much affinity with communism or left wing politics. Some 'suspect' tutors, such as V. Allen,

W. Hamling, H.J. Fyrth and A.T. D'Eye, were subject to rigorous scrutiny, criticised, or even encouraged to seek another job.[43]

In this cold war atmosphere the miltary authorities began to exercise even tighter control over the courses and lectures provided by the RBs for HM Forces. They quite openly debarred communists and others with left wing views, and interfered with what was being taught. They attempted to prohibit the discussion of ideas which even remotely challenged their conservative perspective. McCarthyism predominated in the Services' adult education, and was acceded to (if uneasily) by the RBs.[44]

Towards the end of 1949, the government (in the form of the Colonial Office) took direct action to break the 'Oxford monopoly' in extramural work in Africa because of the anti-colonial and left-wing tendencies of some of its expatriate tutors and T.L. Hodgkin, the Secretary of the Extramural Delegacy. (The Oxford tutors were teaching mainly political subjects which inevitably politicised the African students, and which took on a special significance in the politically-charged atmosphere of West Africa after 1948. Their viewpoint was generally favourable to the independence movements and their teaching undoubtedly gave succour to these movements.)[45] Arthur Creech-Jones, the Secretary of State for the Colonies, decided that 'the tendency to build up an Oxford monopoly of colonial interests in the extramural field should now be resisted', and 'that in view of Mr. Hodgkin's associations we cannot agree to the Oxford Delegacy starting work in E. and C. Africa.'[46] The British Council and other, politically more trustworthy, extramural departments were encouraged to take over the work from Oxford. Over the next few years the Colonial Office also took steps to prevent other communist or anti-colonialist lecturers, including D. Wiseman, J. Rex and M. Barratt-Brown, from taking up extramural posts in Africa.[47]

The net effect of all these incidents was the development of an understanding of what was politically permissible and the defining of boundaries of acceptability beyond which the RBs (whether voluntary movement or professional tutors) were not permitted to stray. There was usually no need for the state to act directly as policeman or censor: the RBs were quite capable of restraining themselves. They undertook their own discreet surveillance of the political attitudes of their classes and their tutors, both through informal internal channels and through more formal class visiting. Where they felt there were risks of undue political offence, they took action. Although it did not occur very frequently, some tutors were certainly disciplined, dismissed or not employed or re-employed because their political beliefs or activities were considered unacceptable.[48] This made tutors very sensitive to what was permissible, and their lack of security of tenure made them particularly susceptible to such pressures. Therefore, for most of the time, the RBs did not need to exercise direct control or take direct action. Being well aware of the ideological limits, tutors imposed their own constraints and kept within them most of the time.[49] They were mostly really well-trained circus dogs.[50]

When the understanding or the training did break down, then the financial relationship between state and RBs did provide for more direct control in the last resort. This did not constitute a heavy-handed censorship, but there was a degree of surveillance and a generally lightly executed controlling influence. This was occasionally exercised directly from Whitehall, but more often indirectly through the HMIs or the LEAs.[51]

The HMIs had an ambivalent role. Often they were friendly and supportive, but they were also required to carry out political investigations. And they did occasionally comment on what they regarded as a politically biased syllabus or suggest that a tutor should correct an alleged political imbalance.[52] The HMIs became more strict in this respect by the late 1930s, when they were given an unequivocal role in political surveillance.[53]

The LEAs showed very little interest in RB adult education for much of the time, but they did succeed, in this period between 1925–50, in establishing the right to 'watch over' RB provision. Many LEAs regarded the payment of grant as entitling (or obliging) them to maintain this watch over RB classes, tutors and syllabuses. They established a variable pattern of representation on the RB committees.[54] For most of the time they carried out their surveillance in a cursory or desultory manner, but it could, and occasionally did, allow them to exercise political influence. For example, when a Conservative-Liberal alliance temporarily captured control of Sheffield City Council in 1932, it stripped the WEA of its grant because of its too-close association with the local Labour Party.[55] In 1933, Bradford Education Committee required the WEA to submit all details about grant-aided courses and their tutors in advance, and to admit LEA officers to the classes 'in order to secure that the classes are conducted to the satisfaction of the Committee.'[56] LEA officials made similar visits to classes in other areas.[57] The Lancashire Education Committee withheld grant aid in respect of particular courses provided by the RBs on a number of occasions during the 1930s, always because they were considered too left wing.[58] The Swansea Education Committee Chairman tried to prevent the appointment of an extramural tutor in 1933[59] and other councillors and LEA officials interfered with the RBs from time to time, if they considered them to be acting subversively.[60] Although there is no evidence that direct LEA controls were often exercised, there were sufficient complaints from LEAs to create an atmosphere of restraint at local level. This atmosphere inevitably contained an element of coercion because it emanated from people who held the purse strings.

The result of all this interference, or influence, whether direct or indirect, was the establishment of an accepted ideological boundary which allowed the RBs (both the voluntary movement and the professionals) to range freely across the broad centre of the British political spectrum, reinforcing a liberal-bourgeois or social-democratic range of values, but relegating Marxist, communist or revolutionary-socialist perspectives to the margins. However, this is not the total picture. There were inevitably some contradictions and tendencies which ran counter to the general trend. As Orwell stated in 1943:

> *No one acquainted with the Government pamphlets, A.B.C.A. lectures, documentary films and broadcasts to occupied countries which have been issued during the past two years imagines that our rulers would sponsor this kind of thing if they could help it. Only, the bigger the machine of government becomes, the more loose ends and forgotten corners there are in it. This is perhaps a small consolation, but it is not a despicable one. It means that in countries where there is already a strong liberal tradition, bureaucratic tyranny can perhaps never be complete. The striped-trousered ones will rule, but so long as they are forced to maintain an intelligentsia, the intelligentsia will have a certain amount of autonomy.*[61]

This residual autonomy is an important part of the overall ideological framework.

One of the more minor contradictions inherent in adult education was that, from time to time, the bureaucrats and civil servants who were supposedly keeping it under control in fact provided protection against political attacks. This was partly because it was in their professional interest to keep the lid on controversies and to shield adult education from the public scrutiny.[62] But it also reflected the fact that adult education was serving a useful political purpose to the state. It needed adult education to provide a bulwark against revolutionism and to act as a liberal magnet to attract potentially subversive working-class intellectuals, just as much as adult education needed government money. This symbiotic relationship gave the RBs a greater degree of independence than their dependence on grant aid would seem to suggest – but only for as long as they served their political purpose!

A second contradictory aspect of the framework within which adult education operated was that grant aid and the consequent regulations (AERs) which were applied to grant-aided classes, while potentially a constraining influence,[63] were also vital to the very existence of liberal adult education. 'Securing . . . direct grant aid was probably Mansbridge's greatest achievement, for without it the tutorial class movement would almost certainly have failed at an early stage.'[64] And without the tutorial classes, the rest of the WEA/extramural provision almost certainly would have withered away (or never started). Having been secured by Mansbridge's masterstroke, the earmarked RB grant and the AERs which required RB adult education to be liberal (i.e. non-vocational) were the guarantors of the survival of liberal adult education. They prevented it from being subsumed into less-liberal (more vocationally orientated or 'economically relevant') sectors of the educational establishment.[65] Thus, the grant and the regulations were both a politically constraining influence and an important protection against illiberal forces.

Another apparent contradiction is to be found in the fact that, although most of the constraints were imposed on left wing tendencies, there were occasional injunctions against fascist, conservative or anti-Soviet bias.[66]

It is also perhaps somewhat contradictory that a predominantly social-democratic adult education movement did not totally exclude a Marxist or communist minority (although coming close to such a position during the cold war). It is less surprising that the role of the communists and the communist party revealed some deep divisions and contradictions within the adult education movement. There is no real concrete evidence of communist propagandising or of a concerted communist party conspiracy to place communists in adult education during this period, but there was a difference in emphasis between communist party officials, who expected some tangible results from the adult education connection, and the communist or Marxist tutors who, like Thomas Hodgkin, generally 'believed that if one taught honestly and seriously and raised basic and serious problems in whatever one was teaching, people would find their own way to Marxism. It was no one's function to indoctrinate people.'[67] Most communist intellectuals' first loyalty was to intellectual integrity, so there was no real conflict of interests in their adult education work. But many regarded it as legitimate that in this work they should introduce Marxist ideas to confront bourgeois ideas in the 'battle of ideas', and to present a Marxist alternative to the orthodox bourgeois perspective. This exposed within the adult education movement a very real difference of opinion about how much prominence it was legitimate to allow to Marxist views. Liberals generally thought it ought to correspond to how prevalent such views already were in society. Adult education should thus reflect rather than challenge the prevailing ideology. Marxists widely considered it was legitimate that they should present their views as a real alternative ideology – seriously to challenge prevailing bourgeois/capitalist views, and thereby present an objective, total picture to the students rather than a one-sided, orthodox one. These very different views of what was permissible or desirable in liberal adult education were not reconcilable, and came into collision during the cold war.[68]

It is perhaps one of the ironies rather than contradictions of the adult education movement that its somewhat cursory treatment of Marxism was partially responsible for the narrow, illiberal nature of English Marxism during this period. Virtually ignored by, if not excluded from, the dialectic of liberal adult education, the study of Marxism was largely confined to a few university scholars and the efforts of the Communist Party and the NCLC, which were heavily influenced by the undemocratic, totalitarian tendencies of Leninism and Stalinism. It is possible that if the study of Marxism had been brought more centrally within the liberal adult education fold, there might have developed an organically working class, autodidactic English Marxist tradition which would have been altogether more liberal and less bolshevist than the version which was fostered by the communist party during the 1920s, 1930s and 1940s.[69]

Another irony was that, despite the much vaunted social purpose of adult education, there is very little evidence of political conversions. Adult education's political influence was very largely confined to confirming existing political convictions. The classes did not so much alter students' views as galvanise them into more activity. Even in this respect, although there is little doubt that it generated a considerable amount of social activism, it reinforced activism as much as it caused it. How much of the social and political activism of those involved in adult education was directly attributable to adult education remains an open question, although it is a reasonable conclusion that many of these activities were influenced by the adult education that was closely associated with them.[70]

The final contradiction is that some of this influence may have had unintended results. In the formulation of its ideological boundaries, the adult education movement very cleverly appeared to be diverting its working class students from a fundamental challenge to the structures, value system and norms of society without imposing an authoritarian censorship. But paradoxically 'such a challenge *may* arise as a result of the effect of education on societal interests'.[71] An educational system cannot necessarily be confined within the limits that are laid down for it. The dialectical process of liberal education must permit all arguments and ideas to be expressed and the best and most powerful to triumph. This means that it is always possible for an ideologically unorthodox perspective to challenge the *status quo*, raise the political consciousness of the students, win the argument, and equip and encourage people to pursue a social purpose very different from the one favoured by the educational providers. It is this Socratic approach – dialectic rather than indoctrinating – that will bring ideological change. 'A tutor can only be a midwife – to help people to develop their own ideas. It is only ideas that you reach by your own process of thinking, however much you have been stimulated by others, that are any good to you.'[72] It is here, within the very kernel of liberalism, that one finds its central paradoxical contradiction – that it must ultimately make room for ideas and an ideology whose strength and power may break its bounds, and eradicate the false consciousness of bourgeois society. With its close affinity to the mainstream British liberal tradition, the adult education movement shared this central contradiction.

Notes and References

1   This article is a revised and expanded version of the concluding chapter of the author's PhD thesis, 'The ideology of English responsible body adult education 1925–1950' (University of Leeds, 1984). The initial research was made possible by the grant of a year's study leave by the University of Leeds and by the award of a research grant by the Leverhulme Trust.

2   Fieldhouse, 1984, pp38–79.

3   R. Terrill, *R.H. Tawney and his Times*, Andre Deutsch, 1974, p277.

4   Fieldhouse, 1984, pp102–8.

5   PRO, ED. 24/1915, Board of Education Minute paper on the relations of the WEA to the LEAs (3 July 1925), para 14.

6   Mary Stocks, *The WEA: the First Fifty Years*, WEA, 1953, p143; E.J. King, 'The relationship between adult education and social attitudes in English industrial society', unpublished PhD thesis, University of London, 1955, p265; F.V. Pickstock, 'Oxford and working class education', unpublished paper presented to the International Graduate Summer School, Oxford (10 August 1978); B. Jennings, *Knowledge is Power: A Short History of the WEA*, University of Hull, 1979, p50.

7   Fieldhouse, 1984, pp136–46.

8   R. Fieldhouse, 'The ideology of English adult education teaching 1925–50', *Studies in Adult Education* 15, 1983, pp11–35.

9   Fieldhouse, 1983.

10 PRO ED. 24/1916, Miss M. Maxse to H. Ramsbotham, 2 November 1932 and Board of Education Minute paper, 9–21 November 1932.

11 Lord Pakenham, *Born to Believe*, Jonathan Cape, 1953, pp59–67 and 79–84.

12 *The Highway* 30, 1937–8, pp98-9 and 31, 1938–9, pp88–90.

13 *The Highway* 30, 1937–8, pp38–46 and 97–100.

14 *The Highway* 31, 1938–9, pp14–15.

15 *The Highway* 30, 1937–8, pp129–32.

16 During the 1930s and immediate post-war period, despite occasional official bouts of suspicion about the activities of certain tutors, there was an overall anti-fascist semblance of unity which gave rise to a general tolerance of political 'unorthodoxy'. It was therefore relatively rare for tutors to be criticised for leftist tendencies. Nevertheless, there were a few complaints – e.g. concerning H.L. Beales who was accused of being not only a socialist but an avowed communist; A.T. D'Eye for being anti-capitalist and pro-Russian; J.R. Armstrong for the bohemian social habits and extreme political views of his associates; James Cameron for advocating communist ideas; R.H.S.Crossman and G.D.H. Cole for their intemperance, socialism and over-zealous commitment to the working class; Maurice Bruce for alleged anti-imperialist tendencies. (See Fieldhouse, 1984, pp207–18.) There were rather more alleged communists or fellow-travellers

amongst civilian lecturers for HM Forces during the war. See, e.g., the cases of J.R. Armstrong; D.N. Pritt; Van der Spenkle; Campbell and Burton; Rosita Forbes; Sir Paul Dukes; S.F. Osiakovski; V.J. Torr; John White; F.A.P. Howe, Diana Levin. (Fieldhouse, 1984, pp541–60). And the witch-hunting became acute during the cold war. (Fieldhouse, 1984, pp233–341 and R. Fieldhouse, *Adult Education and the Cold War: Liberal Values Under Siege 1946–51*, Leeds Studies in Adult and Continuing Education, University of Leeds, forthcoming.

17   PRO T. 161/186/S. 17166, Lord Eustace Percy to Walter Guiness, 7 October 1925.

18   R. Fieldhouse, 'Voluntaryism and the state in adult education: the WEA and the 1925 TUC Education Scheme'. *History of Education* 10, 1981, pp45–63.

19   PRO ED. 24/1915, Lord Eustace Percy to Sir Percy Jackson, 25 September, 1925.

20   J.A. Blyth, *English University Adult Education 1908–1958: A Unique Tradition*, Manchester University Press, 1983, pp77 and 84.

21   PRO ED. 73/38, newspaper cuttings and Board of Education papers relating to the WEA SW District.

22   PRO ED. 24/1916, newspaper cuttings, reports and correspondence relating to a day school on the development of Russian industrialism held at Chatham in April 1933. There is no hard evidence to substantiate the accusation.

23   J.H. Matthews and J.R. Armstrong, interviews and correspondence with author.

24   PRO ED. 80/26, report by HMI Dann on the case of Mary Hickley.

25   PRO ED. 73/1, 11 and 41, HMI reports on Hull University College adult education work, 1933, and Birmingham University and West Midlands WEA adult education, 1934.

26   PRO ED. 80/22, HMI Dann's report on the annual conference of the British Institute of Adult Education, 16–19 September 1938; *The Highway* 30, 1938, pp113–4.

27   PRO ED. 80/22, C.F.R. Bagnall to Brigadier-General H. Clifton-Brown, MP, 5 June 1939.

28   PRO ED. 80/22. It is clear from the evidence that Bagnall was not present at the lecture and that his accusations were based on hearsay, or on what Jardine said at a different place and time, when he lectured to the League of Nations at Newbury some days previously.

29   Lord Wigg, interview with author.

30   PRO ED. 80/26, HMI Jack's brief for Minister of Education R.A. Butler, 14 September 1944.

31   M. Bruce, interview and correspondence with author and 'Reminiscences extramural 1932–41', Cambridge University Library, BEMS 38/31, pp22–3.

32   Bruce.

33   PRO ED. 80/23, Minute paper on Adult Education Controversial Topics, May 1940. The theory of 'federal union' gained some popularity in the 'phoney war' period, as an easy antidote to war. It was based on the assumption that wars arose from the rivalry between sovereign states, and therefore to abolish state sovereignty and replace it by a Federal Union of States would abolish war.

34   PRO ED. 80/23.

35   PRO ED. 80/23.

36   PRO ED. 80/23.

37   PRO ED. 80/23.

38   PRO ED. 80/23.

39   PRO ED. 80/23. There is internal evidence indicating that the CJAC statement was drafted and approved by the Board of Education before it was issued.

40   Fieldhouse, 1984, pp222–6.

41   Fieldhouse, 1984, pp482–587.

42   Fieldhouse, *Adult Education and the Cold War*, Chapters 2 and 3.

43   Fieldhouse, *Adult Education and the Cold War*, Chapter 2.

44   Fieldhouse, *Adult Education and the Cold War*, Chapter 5.

45   Fieldhouse, *Adult Education and the Cold War*, Chapter 4, and R. Fieldhouse, 'Cold war and colonial conflicts in British West African adult education, 1947–53', *History of Education Quarterly* 24, 1984, pp359–68.

46   Rhodes House Library (Oxford), Creech Jones papers, MSS Brit. Emp. S.332, 34/3, ff 34–6.

47   Fieldhouse, *Adult Education and the Cold War*, Chapter 4 and 'Cold war and colonial conflicts in British West African adult education', pp368–9.

48   Fieldhouse, 1984, pp391–414.

49   Fieldhouse, 1984, pp417–20.

50   ' . . . Though there is no definite prohibition . . . official policy is never flouted. Circus dogs jump when the trainer cracks his whip, but the really well-trained dog is the one that turns his somersault when there is no whip . . . ' G. Orwell, *Tribune*, 7 July 1944, quoted in *The Collected Essays, Journalism and Letters of George Orwell*, edited by Sonia Orwell and I. Angus, Vol. 3, Penguin, 1970, pp180–1. Although this comment does not refer to adult education, it reflects exactly the same attitude.

51   Fieldhouse, 1984, pp432–81.

52   Fieldhouse, 1984, pp440–42. For examples of HMI political investigations, see incidents quoted above – the HMIs' comments on the 1925 TUC education scheme; reports on adult education in Yorkshire, Lancashire and Cheshire (1927–8), and the classes provided by Hull and Birmingham (1933–4); and the examination of WEA and extramural tutors in Cambridge in the later 1930s.

53   PRO ED. 80/22, Instructions for the Regulation of Courses (1939) required HMIs to satisfy themselves 'that there is no political propaganda tendency' in courses conducted under the Adult Education Regulations.

54   Fieldhouse, 1984, pp458–65.

55   G. Brown, 'Independence and incorporation: the Labour College Movement and the WEA before the Second World War', in Jane Thompson (ed) *Adult Education for a Change*, Hutchinson, 1980, p114.

56   PRO ED. 73/42, list of conditions which Bradford Education Committee imposed in respect of grant aid to the WEA (1933).

57   E.g. Nottingham extramural area. E. Eagle, interview with author.

58   A.J. Allaway, interview with author.

59   PRO ED. 73/47, papers relating to the appointment of Dr Illtyd David.

60   E.g. in Staffordshire, Kent, Sussex and Devon: Fieldhouse, 1984, pp468–9.

61   G. Orwell, *Poetry and the Microphone* (1943), quoted in *The Collected Essays, Journalism and Letters of George Orwell*, Vol 2, pp381–2.

62   E.g. Board of Education officials decided in 1934 to suppress a passage in an HMI's report which cast 'a rather livid light on … Adult Education classes', for fear that if the report 'ever got into the hands of the uninitiated or unsympathetic, this passage might supply popular material for attack on Adult Education work in general.' (PRO ED. 73/1, Board of Education Minute paper referring to HMI reports on Birmingham University and West Midlands WEA classes.)

63   Fieldhouse, 1984, pp433–6; S.G. Raybould, *The English Universities and Adult Education*, WEA, 1951, pp92–116.

64   R. Fieldhouse, *The WEA: Aims and Achievements 1903–1977*, Syracuse University, 1977, p17.

65   R. Taylor, K. Rockhill and R. Fieldhouse, *University Adult Education in Britain and the U.S.A.*, Croom Helm, 1985, particularly pp 18–19 and 62–77.

66   E.g. The allegations that the Oxford part-time tutor, S. Schofield, showed an antagonism towards Russia in 1942–3; and that the WEA was used for the furtherance of anti-labour propaganda by providing lectures for the Blaydon-on-Tyne Rent and Ratepayers Association in 1946. (See Fieldhouse, 1984, pp225–7.)

67   T.L. Hodgkin, interview with author. For a detailed analysis of the role of the Communist Party in adult education, see Fieldhouse, *Adult Education and the Cold War*, Chapter 2.

68   Fieldhouse, *Adult Education and the Cold War*.

69   For further examination of this hypothesis, see S. MacIntyre, *A Proletarian Science*, Cambridge University Press, 1980, and J. Rée, *Proletarian Philosphers*, Clarendon Press, 1984.

70   Fieldhouse, 1984 pp 146–52, 376–9 and 645–53.

71   J.E. Thomas, *Radical Adult Education; Theory and Practice*, Nottingham University. 1982, p5.

72   Hodgkin, interview with author.

10

Gender and Education: A study of the ideology and practice of community based women's education

GILLIAN HIGHET
(Studies in the Education of Adults, 18, 1986.)

Gender and the Education Debate

It is only recently that gender has been taken seriously within the education debate and that educational inequalities based on sex division have been identified as a major characteristic of the British education system. Comprehensive co-education has come to be regarded as the cornerstone of the rhetoric enshrining the ideal of equal educational opportunity for all, despite evidence that it is likely to disadvantage girls academically. This tendency is reflected in many different aspects of the school system with corresponding effects on the distribution of life chances.

Language itself has been shown to provide perhaps the clearest example of how at the deepest but least intentional level teaching often conveys the impression that men, and only men, are the initiators, innovators and active agents of human life.[1] Similarly, it has been demonstrated that the content of the curriculum and text books continues to contribute to a diminution of women's contribution to society.[2] The organisation of the school and the government of education in general also share responsibility for contributing to the process of gender differentiation.[3] An examination of the characteristics of the curricular 'free choice' which operates in many schools has also provided evidence which supports the contention that girls are still being consistently and systematically discriminated against.[4] Other factors, such as the attitude and behaviour of teachers, and social constraints, have also been shown to play a significant role in this process.[5]

The cumulative effect of such factors is to reinforce the logic of the sexual division of labour and equip young women to take their 'rightful' and 'natural' place within the sexual hierarchy. However, it is not only within the school system that this process operates.

Traditionally, women have consistently been involved in liberal adult education and other post-compulsory educational opportunities in large numbers. However, evidence suggests that the practices and ideology of such provision have combined to reinforce traditional assumptions which are counterproductive in terms of women's progress towards equality.[6] To a great extent, it is as appendages of homes, husbands and children that the vast majority of women are catered for. The net effect of such provision is that women are still being socialised into accepting different and unequal roles from those of men. Continuing education opportunities for women, therefore, still appear to a large extent to be contributing to the reproduction of sexual divisions in society and the perpetuation of relative female under-achievement at all levels of societal structures. In addition to the ideological control exerted over women, it is also the case that the majority of continuing education opportunities are not geared in a practical sense to women's needs, particularly in relation to child care responsibilities.[7] A recent publication includes amongst its recommendations for an improved community education service in Scotland the need for priority to be given to 'women, particularly young married women with small children'.[8]

It would appear, then, that women continue to be discriminated against not only within schooling, but also within other formal educational structures. However, other less formal forums for learning are beginning to spring up and there has been a mushrooming of interest in community-based women's education in Scotland over the last few years. Such projects take place in local communities, often in peripheral housing schemes with few facilities, and offer an opportunity for women who would not otherwise be likely to seek any further involvement in education after leaving school. Such provision has other advantages – learning opportunities are offered at a time and place suitable to the participants themselves in an informal setting, and are usually free. In addition, the approach is flexible and responsive to the needs and suggestions of the women involved. Furthermore, although the activities are worthwhile in themselves, they can also potentially be a vehicle for raising confidence and self-esteem and may facilitate a process of personal change and growth and the exploration of new opportunities. Such provision would therefore appear to offer women a unique opportunity to participate in shared learning with other women – learning which has the potential to lead towards a clearer examination of women's social and economic roles, generating new knowledge and action from a female perspective.

Some research indicates, however, that there is little evidence 'of any critical examination of the assumption and practice of community education as it relates to females'.[9] Much of the form and content of existing programmes, it would seem, has been incorporated by restrictive stereotypes with a focus on topics such as child rearing, cookery and keep fit. This suggests that such provision, in common with other post compulsory educational opportunities, also contributes to the socialisation of women into accepting different and unequal societal roles from those of men.

If this is indeed the case, there is strong justification for arguing that educators have a responsibility to examine the nature and content of such provision to ensure that curricula, methods of organisation, and so on, actively undermine traditional restrictive and discriminatory roles for women. It was with this task in mind that it was decided to embark upon a small research project based in the city of Glasgow. The main purpose of the study was to examine whether, and if so to what extent, a selected sample of women's informal community education programmes was still contributing to the socialisation of women into accepting differential societal roles. In the interests of preserving anonymity and privacy the groups observed will not be named but instead have been designated with appropriate initials and will be referred to in this manner throughout the article.

Community Based Women's Education in Practice

Three women's educational groups – CAG, PWG and AWAG – were selected on the basis of having different geographical and socio-economic characteristics. Of the three groups, the first two are supported by mainstream community education, and the third by a voluntary organisation. (Since the implementation of the recommendations of the Alexander Report, adult education in Scotland has been the function of the community education service which operates under the auspices of the appropriate local government agency – in this case Strathclyde Regional Council). All three groups have an average membership of around ten.

The first stage of the research involved conducting a structured interview with the front line provider of each of the groups. This was designed to discover to what extent the workers involved have adopted a position which opposes the dominant culture of present society as it relates to women and to what extent they have developed alternative goals and values in women's education and identified means by which these might be achieved. The next stage involved a period of participatory observation during which several meetings of each of the groups were attended. In the course of the observation attention was paid to the environment and the general atmosphere, methods, content, type of management, degree of participation, relationships within the group, etc. in order to discover the various ways in which these factors affected the learning process. Finally, an informal interview was held with two members of each of the groups, the two women being selected on the basis that they provided a representative view of the group as a whole. The primary purpose of the interview was to find out how far the women themselves, as a result of their involvement with their particular group, have developed an alternative understanding of women's traditional role in society and how far they regard community based women's educational programmes as a vehicle for challenging and undermining the restrictive and discriminatory functions traditionally assigned to them.

All of the material obtained by these methods was then organised and evaluated in a way which facilitated the emergence of a network of factors, the interaction of which seemed to be responsible for the various ways in which the three groups have evolved and developed. It was then possible to use this analysis to provide an overview of the extent to which the learning outcomes of this sort of provision are still bound by traditional restrictive stereotypes. Finally, it was possible to make suggestions and recommendations relating to how community educators can provide effective educational programmes which will undermine and challenge traditional assumptions about women's role in society.

Six major factors have been identified, the cumulative effects of which appear to have been largely responsible for shaping the development of the three groups. These factors are:

(1) socio-economic and cultural background
(2) interpersonal relationships
(3) relationships with children
(4) nature of the curriculum
(5) organisational structure and methods
(6) role of the worker.

CAG

This group operates within a community characterised by a very high level of adult unemployment, poor social conditions and a high degree of relative poverty. CAG itself is composed mainly of lone parents and the general trend seems to be one of unsatisfactory or abandoned relationships with men. All of these conditions have combined to produce a group of women who uncritically accept their traditional role. They tend to define themselves solely in terms of their function as mothers for it is within this role that they achieve status. These factors perhaps help to explain why the majority of their activities are geared towards providing for the needs of their children, rather than their own needs as individuals.

The socio-economic characteristics of CAG also have important effects on relationships within the group and attitudes towards their children. The group is extremely divided and in a constant state of conflict. It may be that the poor social conditions and high rate of unemployment have led to a community characterised by in-fighting and conflicts of interest rather than one united by a sense of solidarity and a common aim to improve conditions for the mutual benefit of all. This has grave implications for the effectiveness of learning groups like CAG. The fact that all the women live near one another and see each other frequently may also contribute to this trend. This perhaps makes it difficult to see things in an objective light and hence the women cannot seem to settle their differences. It should be noted, however, that close and frequent proximity need not necessarily result in conflict and alienation. Given a different set of circumstances it could well have the opposite effect of promoting harmony and solidarity. So far as CAG is concerned, however, it does appear that this factor may be adding to their difficulties given the conflicts and rivalry that already clearly exist.

Relationships with children are a significant factor to be considered in relation to women's education, particularly with regard to the implications for good creche provision. CAG, in common with the other two groups, has no organised creche and instead the members have chosen to supervise the children themselves. This clearly influences the effectiveness and extent of the learning that is able to take place. What is particularly significant is the apparent lack of interest in establishing a creche. This seems to be largely due to the nature of relationships with children, characterised as they are by fierce protectiveness and uncritical acceptance of their function as child carers. It may be that the women in this particular group either suffer deeply embedded guilt or anxiety about leaving their children with someone else or that they share traditional assumptions that child care is low priority, low status, and ultimately the responsibility of the mother.

The nature of CAG's activities clearly represents another significant factor. The majority of their activities are closely related to providing for the needs of children – summer playschemes, girls' club, and so on. This factor, however, should not be considered in isolation. It would be quite wrong to assume that such activities could not potentially be useful in promoting discussion about women's role in society. However, so far as CAG is concerned, the nature of these activities, together with other factors which influence the group, seem to have combined to ensure that an awareness of women's traditional role in society has not had the opportunity to emerge, far less be challenged and undermined.

The organisational structure of this group also seems to be significant. CAG, unlike the other two groups, is run by a committee of appointed office bearers. Although decisions are ostensibly made by consensus, there is some evidence to suggest that decisions are sometimes arbitrarily overturned by individuals, thus creating conflict. This sort of structure does not seem to be appropriate for CAG as its hierarchical nature appears to have contributed to the development of power struggles within the group. Another significant feature of CAG's structure is that it is composed of individuals some of whom attend every afternoon, others only on certain afternoons (CAG meets five afternoons per week). It is therefore very difficult for the women to perceive the group as a single unit and it is very likely that this has contributed to its divisive nature.

So far as methods are concerned, the overall pattern is that apart from occasional discussion and planning of future events CAG's meetings are mainly devoted to social chat. It is clear that active participation within the local community and the achievements the group has shown itself to be capable of in the past have led to increased confidence and a growth of self-esteem. However, it does seem that the failure of the group to provide opportunities for systematic learning to take place has meant that there is little chance to broaden horizons, develop new insights and increase knowledge.

The role of the worker attached to CAG is clearly a crucial factor requiring investigation. The way in which the worker perceives her duties and responsibilities towards the group has had a significant effect on the nature and degree of effectiveness of her role. It would appear that she perceives herself more as a facilitator, advisor and resource person than someone who is actively committed to developing and specifying alternative goals and values in women's education and identifying ways in which these can be achieved. This perception of her role is in apparent contradiction with her view of community-based women's education in general which she considers to be a potential vehicle for facilitating an awareness of women's role in society and for helping to redress the balance. It would appear that the worker's positive attitude is not reflected in what is actually happening in CAG. One reason for this may be a failure to confront the issue of aims and objectives. Although the worker is aware that stated objectives are not being met, she has not approached this situation by re-examining these in the light of the problems the group is experiencing. As a result, although conditions within the group have altered dramatically, the objectives have remained unchanged, thus contributing to the discontent and disharmony. It may be that crisis intervention is an inappropriate strategy for this group and that a more systematic approach, including regular intervention where appropriate and informal ongoing evaluation, is required. Above all, it would appear that the worker's ideological commitment must be reflected in her practice.

PWG

The socio-economic background against which PWG operates is significantly different from that which characterises CAG. Although living in a designated Area of Priority Treatment, the members of this group are not subject to extreme financial pressures since most are married with husbands in employment. Since most of the women continue to live within the context of relationships with men they do not, to the same extent as the women in CAG, appear to derive their status purely from their function as mothers. The fact that they are able to afford a social life outwith the home probably also contributes to this. Thus, involvement with this group appears to provide opportunities for increasing the women's potential to enjoy a satisfying life outwith the confines of home and family.

PWG, which meets one afternoon per week, has managed, unlike CAG, to develop a real sense of solidarity within the group. It is perhaps because the women are not totally dependent upon the group and each other's company, since they derive at least some satisfaction from aspects of their family and other relationships, that they have been able to achieve this friendly sharing atmosphere. The fact that are not so severely affected by the effects of poverty and poor social conditions may also have contributed. What is very clear, whatever the reasons for this, is that this sort of atmosphere is very conducive to learning and this has been borne out by the learning outcomes and achievements of PWG.

In common with the two other groups, PWG does not have an organised creche and this has clearly affected the extent and effectiveness of learning. It is significant, however, that PWG was actively involved in trying to set up a creche. A crucial factor here seems to be the way in which the women view their role as mothers and subsequently the sort of relationships they have with their children. The women in PWG exhibited an awareness of the benefits of a well-run creche and the positive effect this is likely to have on the learning process. They were clearly also aware of the potential for good creche facilities to restore to women the knowledge that they have not ceased to exist as individuals and can function in situations apart from the traditional ones of housework and child-care. It would appear that such insights have been able to emerge largely because the women in PWG are not fiercely protective towards their children and do not uncritically accept their traditional function as child carers.

The activities in which PWG is involved are almost exclusively health-related. Although the topic of health itself is not directly related to women's socio-economic position, it does seem to lend itself very easily to an exploration of this wider issue. Indeed, it is clear that PWG uses health issues not only as a way of improving knowledge but also as a vehicle for facilitating discussion and the development of an awareness of the discriminatory nature of society and how this affects women's lives.

The way in which PWG is run also seems to be conducive to effective learning. The group operates as a democratic structureless body with no formal committee procedure and decision making is by consensus. This way of operating has made it easy for all the women to participate in the decision making process and this has resulted in the development of an awareness of their abilities in this area and a corresponding growth in confidence. Since no one holds an official position the climate is not conducive to power struggles developing and the harmonious atmosphere makes it easier for effective learning to take place. It cannot be assumed, however, that absence of structure will necessarily always result in a harmonious atmosphere. It may be the other way around, namely, that a harmonious atmosphere may allow for effective operation without structure. This issue is obviously a complex one requiring closer examination, but whichever is the more relevant in the case of PWG, the effects are certainly beneficial to the learning process.

The approach and methods of PWG also differ significantly with corresponding effects on the group's development. Meetings are generally allocated to the discussion of specific topics or to Open University short course work and this often involves inviting a guest speaker. These sessions generally involve participation by everyone and this process, together with the sharing of experiences in a systematic way, has led to increased confidence which is expressed not only within the group but also in situations outside. Since all this is largely organised and implemented by the women themselves, without the assistance of the worker, the general level of self-esteem has risen accordingly.

The role of the worker has also clearly benefited the development of PWG. The worker involved is well aware of the limitations and discriminatory nature of traditional educational provision for women and of the potential of informal community based women's educational groups to undermine and challenge this trend. Her objectives for the group were arrived at in consultation with the women themselves and are largely being achieved in practice. It is for this reason that the worker has withdrawn to a large extent over recent months and has elected to play more of a facilitating role. This has probably contributed to the growth in confidence of the women to define their own learning needs and in the development of an awareness of their own capabilities. However, if the group is going to extend its influence by attracting more women and getting actively involved in issues of relevance to women within the community – an objective shared by both the worker and at least some of the women – it may be that more constructive intervention would be useful.

AWAG

The low status of the Asian community as a whole and the inequality of provision of welfare benefits, social services and the like are two factors which have contributed in a significant way to the direction this group has taken and the issues to which it has given priority. AWAG has therefore become active within the community in a way which provides practical help and assistance to Asian women in relation to the problems they face as an ethnic minority group. Cultural factors also clearly affect the way Asian women view their role in society. The patriarchal nature of Asian society has inevitably resulted in an uncritical acceptance by the vast majority of Asian women of their appointed role within the family and society as a whole. It should be noted that such characteristics are also in evidence within the context of Scottish working-class culture. The significant point is that there are recognisable differences of degree in the extent to which they are exhibited. Thus, such characteristics tend to appear in a more pervasive and extensive form within the Asian community, hence the continued existence of such a male dominated ideology and the subsequent lack of opportunity for women to challenge it. Thus, the activities of AWAG do not set out to challenge the existing division of roles within the Asian community. Rather, their work is directed towards improving their status and quality of life within their traditional spheres as wives and mothers.

AWAG has succeeded to a considerable extent in developing an atmosphere of loyalty and solidarity, probably largely because of its unique position as an ethnic minority within a dominant Western culture. This harmonious atmosphere is clearly partly a reflection of the recognition that the only way to improve their status and raise the general quality of life is to work together as a community. The relationships within AWAG reflect this necessity and the success of the group is a testament to what can be achieved by people working together for a common cause. The members of AWAG are also aware of the particular hardships facing Asian women as a group, especially in relation to isolation and poor welfare provision, and this factor has also contributed to the building up of solidarity within the group.

It is clear that the women in AWAG are very protective towards their children and accept without question their traditional role, a characteristic shared with the women in CAG. The high degree of protectiveness is probably derived from an acute desire to shield the children from the racial abuse and harassment to which they must occasionally be exposed, or an attempt to compensate for it. The women in AWAG have therefore shown no real interest in establishing a properly run creche since they are largely unaware of the benefits for their learning, preoccupied as they are with protecting their children and fulfilling their maternal roles.

The activities of AWAG primarily address themselves to problems of a racial and cultural origin and it is within these areas that most discussions are confined. However, the sort of issues that AWAG concerns itself with – welfare and social security provision, housing conditions, etc. – are issues that are potentially of concern to all women living together in working-class communities and it may be that, given time, this group may develop a sense of solidarity with all women in the community, and in so doing, start to become aware of the specific problems that face all women in society because of the restrictive, discriminatory role assigned to them. However, so long as the dominant white community and the relevant authorities remain insensitive to the plight of ethnic minority groups living amongst them, it is perhaps unlikely that groups like AWAG would give high priority to women-related issues.

The organisational structure of AWAG is very similar to that of PWG and, as in the previous case, this way of operating has made it easy for all the women to participate in the decision making process and has led to a growth in confidence and general self esteem. The approach and methods of AWAG, however, differ significantly from those of the other two groups. It is the only group which relies upon the worker to attend and lead most of the meetings. These are mostly taken up by discussions centred round the planning and implementation of future events and activities, although on occasion more structured sessions on specific topics are held, sometimes with visiting speakers. The worker also meets with a few key activists in the group between meetings to ensure that decisions are implemented. This sort of systematic, task-centred approach means that the women are actively involved at many different levels and their self esteem and level of confidence have been raised as a result. Such an approach would seem to be consistent with the aims and objectives of the group, and the ongoing support of the worker has ensured that the process of learning by doing is a systematic, continuous one.

It is clear that the worker, through constant support and encouragement, has played a significant role in raising the group's confidence, facilitating an awareness of its capabilities and maximising the effectiveness of learning that has taken place. It is also clear, however, that the direction AWAG has taken and the approach it has adopted reflect the philosophy and ideology of the voluntary agency which employs the worker. Similarly, the issues the group has become involved in also reflect the areas that are given priority by the agency. Thus, their activities have been primarily concerned with minimising the detrimental effects of their status as an ethnic minority group within a dominant Western culture through a process of self-help and community action. The women in AWAG have not, however, been given the opportunity of exploring the issue of the differential gender roles assigned to men and women and therefore have not to any great extent developed an awareness of the sexual discrimination which all women in society are subject to. This is largely because the worker has not adopted an ideological position which opposes the dominant model in relation to the way it affects women's lives. The goals and values she has specified in terms of women's education are not actively geared towards challenging and undermining women's traditional role. The worker's lack of commitment to the potential use of women's educational groups for drawing attention to the sexual inequality that characterises our society would therefore appear to be a significant factor in the group's development.

Towards More Effective Programmes for Women's Education

A thorough analysis of all the material suggests that out of the three programmes studied, only one, PWG, is making a conscious, determined effort to address the problem of the socialisation of women into accepting traditional, discriminatory and restrictive roles in society and attempting to redress the balance. AWAG has addressed itself primarily to problems of a racial and cultural origin rather than exploring gender-based discrimination. This emphasis reflects the reality of the nature of the main problems facing ethnic-minority cultures and the group can boast considerable achievements in this area. The third group, CAG, is experiencing severe internal problems which not only undermine the group's effectiveness but may also threaten its existence. Educational provision for this group has largely failed to facilitate an awareness of the ways in which society discriminates against women, and the women themselves seem to accept uncritically their functions as the home-makers and child-carers of society.

There are clearly many lessons to be learned from the different experiences of these three groups, not least a recognition that the way in which any educational group develops will inevitably be the result of the interaction of a complex set of factors. The task facing educators is that of providing effective educational programmes which will undermine and challenge traditional assumptions about women's role in society, and this can only be achieved by taking due account of all the factors which are likely to contribute to the direction groups take and the degree of effectiveness of the learning which is able to take place.

One crucial factor that has emerged concerns the actual role of community educators and the dilemma they face over this issue. Community educators in general have been trained to adopt a 'facilitating' role, leaving people free to participate in learning of their own choice and to build their own educational provision. Using this model, any under-achievement can be understood in terms of women's failure to capitalise on educational provision by choosing to perceive their futures as wives and mothers, part-time unskilled workers, and so on. From this perspective, the community educator's role is to intervene less in learning programmes and leave people free to choose. However, it has to be recognised that women do not choose to have less education, more unskilled jobs and lower pay than men. The real issue is that they can only choose from the range of options presented to them in education, and so long as sex stereotyping, sexist knowledge and gender differentiation remain common features of educational provision, no women can be said to have 'choice'.

It is clear that the sexual, racial and class divisions which persist in educational practice do not reflect the differential talents and interests of individuals, but rather, reflect the fact that education exists within an ideological framework which justifies disadvantage and makes it seem reasonable and natural. The experiences of the women in CAG, in particular, seem to support this argument, and there is strong justification for insisting that community educators have a responsibility to ensure that our women's educational provision does not contribute to the reproduction of gender divisions in society – by playing a more interventionist role where appropriate. Community educators must therefore adopt an ideological position which opposes the dominant culture of present society as it relates to women. This will also involve developing and specifying alternative goals and values in women's education and identifying means by which these might be achieved.

Another area of concern is the need for better creche facilities. However, the sort of relationships which many women have with their children, and the attitudes they hold in relation to their responsibilities towards children, as illustrated in both CAG and AWAG, often make it difficult to convince women themselves of the importance of creche provision. There is obviously a lot of scope, therefore, for more resources, energy and thought on the part of community educators to be directed towards educating women about the benefits of a well-run creche. The provision of good creche facilities represents a validation of all women's lives – a recognition of the fact that most women spend at least some time engaged in full time child care. It is also an affirmation that women need not suspend all other development while their children are very young. It is therefore potentially very important for community educators to confront the issue of women's reluctance to establish good creche provision and facilitate an awareness of the substantial benefits to be gained.

All three groups observed in this study are very small, often having fewer than ten regular attenders, and this seems to be a fairly common characteristic of groups of this sort. It is obviously impossible and undesirable to fix hard and fast rules about the size of groups, but it does seem that it could well be of benefit in a number of ways to attract more women along. Not only would this increase the wealth of experience within groups, it would also potentially offer greater opportunities to extend their influence within the community. There are various tried and tested ways of publicising groups and attracting new members. These include the use of posters, leaflets, local radio and local newspapers. However, one crucial factor which has to be taken into account when devising appropriate and effective publicity is the probable traditional resistance of women living in working-class communities to post-compulsory educational opportunities. For this reason, extensive outreach work including in-depth interviews is probably the most direct and powerful method and, although time consuming, it is also possible by this method to build up a network of local contacts. Another potentially useful approach might be to organise a specific event or sampler courses in order to inform people of the social and educational opportunities available and give them a chance to determine their own interests and abilities.

Finally, the work of community educators involved in women's education is seriously hampered by the lack of appropriate training opportunities. It has been established that many different factors can affect how women learn and how groups develop, and problems will inevitably arise in situations where some aspects of the learning environment are inappropriate or where certain factors have not been taken account of. Regular workshops, training weekends, where community educators can get together and share experiences and problems with a view to devising appropriate alternative strategies and approaches to women's education could potentially be a very valuable exercise. This would not only facilitate the development of a greater awareness of problems and possible solutions, it would also potentially aid in the construction of a regional and perhaps national network of women's education groups. Thus, instead of operating from positions of isolation, community educators would be able to benefit from each other's mutual support and to some extent make specific knowledge, skills and resources more widely available.

References

1   C. Miller and K. Swift. *Words and Women*, Pelican, 1979, p 5; A. Rich, 'Taking women students seriously' and 'When we dead awaken: writing as re-vision' in A. Rich. *On*

Lies, Secrets and Silences, Virago, 1980, p 241 and p 39; D. Spender. 'Disappearing tricks' in D. Spender and E. Sarah (eds), *Learning to Lose – Sexism and Education*, Women's Press, 1980, pp 165–166.

2   L. Davies and R. Meighan, 'A review of schooling and sex roles with particular reference to the experience of girls in secondary schools' *Education Review* 27, 1975; D. Spender, *Feminist Theorists*, Women's Press, 1983, p 2; M. B. Sutherland, *Sex Bias in Education*, Oxford: Basil Blackwell, 1981, pp 114–120; J. Thompson, *Learning Liberation: Women's Response to Men's Education*, Croom Helm, 1983, p 36.

3   E. Byrne, *Women and Education*, Tavistock, 1978, p 218; I. Payne, 'Sexist ideology and education' in Spender and Sarah, p 35.

4   R. Deem, *Schooling for Women's Work*, RKP, 1980, p 19; Department of Education and Science, *Curricular Differences for Boys and Girls*, Education Survey 21, HMSO, 1975; M. Stanworth, *Gender and Schooling: A Study of Sexual Divisions in the Classroom*, Hutchinson in association with the Explorations in Feminism Collective, 1983, pp 18–19.

5   K. Clarricoates, 'Dinosaurs in the classroom: a re-examination of some aspects of the hidden curriculum in primary schools', *Women's Studies International Quarterly* 1, 1978; Stanworth, p 18; Sutherland, pp 215–219; J. Whyte, 'Sex typing in schools', in A. Kelly (ed), *The Missing Half*, Manchester University Press, 1981, p 267.

6   G. Blunden, 'Vocational education for women's work in England and Wales' in S. Acker, J. Megarry, S. Nisbet, E. Hoyle (eds), *Women and Education*, Kegan Paul, 1984, pp 161–162; N. Keddie, 'Adult education: an ideology of individualism' in J. Thompson (ed), *Adult Education For A Change*, Hutchinson, 1980, pp 55–56.

7   A. Miller, 'The need for good creche facilities for women's education', WEA North of Scotland District, 1984, p 2.

8   D. Alexander, T. Leach and T. Steward, 'Community education, leisure and recreation in three Scottish regions' (Research Summary 1), Scottish Community Education Council, 1984, p 45.

9   A. Bruce, 'What is women's education?' unpublished paper, 1983, p 6 (based on an unpublished thesis by the same author, 'Dominant ideologies in women's education and the search for alternative paradigms').

11

Constructing the Other: Minorities, the state and adult education in Europe

SALLIE WESTWOOD
(Studies in the Education of Adults, 21, 1989.)

This paper is a very preliminary attempt to engage with the comparative method, not methodologically but to step back further to consider some of the premises that underlie our attempts to generate a comparative adult education. It is not intended to undermine our efforts but to be a work of deconstruction which provides a starting point for further discussions. It is necessarily schematic and at times unformed because it grapples with the hidden and moves towards the unknown. But, it is work that is essential if we are to develop a critical inquiry removed from the excesses of positivist social science. Once racism, minorities, ethnicities are foregrounded different trajectories for the comparative project are opened up and demand exploration. It is to some of these themes that I now turn.

The State of the Nation

The engagement with comparative work has too easily and simply been understood as an engagement with cross-national comparisons – the examples of this type of work are numerous. At a commonsense level this seems plausible and at an inter-agency level it seems essential. But, once we invoke nations, we highlight not the commonly assumed geographical inertia of state boundaries but a terrain of struggle and one that is fought over throughout Europe. To consider the question of the position of minorities in the European states opens up the terrain of nations, nationalism and national identities. Nations, on the other hand, assume closure and exclusion. To speak of nations is to invoke 'imagined communities'[1] that, nevertheless are powerful 'and not a bit less real because they are symbolic'.[2] Gramsci's analysis of ideological hegemony helps us to understand the ways in which 'the nation' is constructed through a consensus around 'the people'.[3] In Britain this has been underpinned by the rise of an authoritarian populism which promotes a little Englander mentality and by so doing emphasises homogeneity in British culture. It is an exclusionary account which presents those outside as 'others'. History is rewritten to promote homogeneity and to ignore the diversity and heterogeneity that has marked British culture throughout. There is a pressing need for an account of nations which, rather than deny, celebrates diversity through history and across regions. Attempts have been made in Britain to support this through the development of multi-cultural and anti-racist education which have been supported through the local state in particular locations. Against this are those who support the views recently expressed by the minister for education, Kenneth Baker who, in his speech to the Conservative party conference emphasised 'traditional values' and the importance of children learning the main events of British history. He said, 'Well, I'm not ashamed of our history. Britain has given many great things to the world. That's been our civilising mission.' He went on to emphasise, '. . . the spread of Britain's influence for good throughout the Empire in the 18th and 19th centuries.'[4] The resonances with colonial discourses are very clear, the civilising mission, Empire and Britain as benign and more so, as epochs to be celebrated.

This account of Britain's colonial past relies on a re-working of familiar colonial discourses which subjugated colonial peoples at home and throughout the world. These discourses are not peculiar to Britain but are a shared history throughout Europe. They created an exclusionary language which privileged difference and this difference was marked by subordination to Europe, culturally, economically and politically. The language used to describe the world demonstrates this – the middle East, the far East, the Orient – and the language that was created to socially construct peoples. The term 'Asian', for example, was created by the British to designate peoples of very diverse origins from India and what became Pakistan and now Bangladesh. It is not possible to pursue this here but it is elegantly excavated in the work of Edward Said on orientalism[5] and has been recently explored for India by Inden.[6] The discourses which produced 'the Orient' contained within them a construction of 'the other' which was predicated upon 'fixity' which promoted and sustained stereotypes that remain part of European cultures today. But, as Homi Bhabha notes: 'Fixity as the sign of cultural/historical/racial difference in the discourse of colonialism, is a paradoxical mode of representation: it connotes rigidity and an unchanging order as well as disorder, degeneracy and daemonic repetition.'[7] The contradictions in colonial discourses did not prevent them from becoming hegemonic accounts and it is this legacy with which the comparative project must engage if it is not to be trapped within these discourses. The current work within subaltern studies[8] is an attempt to both deconstruct colonial discourses and to engage in recovery – the recovery of the other, of the colonial knowing subject. Similarly, current work on nations and in Britain on Britishness are an excavation of both past and current discourses that position subjects. These are vital projects and form part of the attempt to actively counter racism and to reconstruct our accounts of ourselves.

The legacy of racism is part of everyday lives, part of the commonsense of European cultures demonstrated in the language, the jokes alongside the institutional practices of societies which are promoted and reproduced by national and local states. But racism, as Gilroy reminds us, '. . . is not a unitary event based on psychological aberration nor some historical antipathy to blacks. . . . It must be understood as a process.'[9] As I have argued:

> *The process to which Gilroy refers is characterised by prejudice and discrimination against groups of people understood to share common racial heritages. Racism rests, in part, upon the mistaken belief that there are biologically distinct races in nature and that, therefore, people have natural attributes determined by their racial origins. Implicit in racism is the idea that one race is culturally superior to another and is, therefore, justified in exercising political and economic dominance.[10]*

The colonial discourses that presented European culture as superior and that through their colonial administrations set about classifying 'races' are still present in the latter part of the twentieth century. The power of these accounts shows the ways in which the state in Britain, for example, treats black Britons not as British but as immigrants reinforcing the distance between black and white while simultaneously maintaining the legacy of Empire, projecting it into the present. Thus, nationhood and national identities are neither simple nor fixed and are currently the site of struggles throughout Europe.

Citizenship

Central to our understandings of state and nation are the discourses that surround citizenship and that have been part of the European tradition of political thought. The battles on this terrain have had revolutionary and reformist outcomes and are currently on the agenda again as the consensus in European political life is further fractured. In Britain the rise of enterprise culture and its promotion as the new ideological hegemonic has far-reaching consequences for conceptions of social justice and a redistributive model of social and economic life. At the heart of this change are the changing conceptions of citizenship. The nineteenth century saw working-class struggles to overcome property qualifications that denied the mass of the population a role as voters in representative democracy and the twentieth century saw the struggles by women for the vote. Each state had a specific trajectory and in each case the struggle for votes was related to rights to collective representation, not just through parties but through workers' unions and other forms of organisations. Civil liberties, the legal rights of persons in relation to the state were and are not given but the outcomes of struggles. The position of minorities has warranted special attention and continues to do so. But, it is not just at the level of legal rights that disenfranchisement may occur, the issues are more complex and relate in part to the relationship between democracy and capitalism. Crucial to the ability to exercise citizenship rights in capitalism is the ability to exchange labour power for wages, to be recognised as a worker. Racism and sexism intervene in this relationship because workers are gendered and they face a racialised employment structure. The statistics in Britain and across Europe point to high levels of unemployment among specific sections of the labour force and black people are over-represented at all ages. With the rise of enterprise culture and the coming together in official discourse of the consumer and the citizen, the one who will exercise choices through money power, the unwaged – whether unemployed, elderly, disabled or single parents – with no options but state benefits begin to have a different relationship with democracy and citizen rights.

Citizenship and the exercise of rights under the law requires knowledge and the relationship between knowledge and power is underlined in any consideration of citizenship. Historically, adult education has had a role in education for citizenship and in Britain this was foregrounded in the famous *1919 Report*. It represents one strand in the complex that makes up adult education and is currently discussed within the broader framework of political education. There is an important role for educators here because without knowledge that allows for the exercise of rights individuals can be disenfranchised. Consequently, civil liberties are an essential part of the agenda of adult education – not only in relation to immigration and nationalities law but more broadly. In this way there is a role for adult education in empowerment.

Culture

There are especially complex issues surrounding the ways in which 'culture' is positioned in the discourses of both the ethnic relations literature as it has developed in Europe and in the works of comparative adult education. In the latter culture remains unspoken, a hidden element subordinated to nation states. But, there is a powerful transfer to the assumptions surrounding nations – that nations come with homogeneous cultures located with national identities. As I have pointed out in the discussion of nations it is an assumption we should, as comparativists, dispense with if we are to move away from empiricist accounts of social and economic formations. While comparative adult education may have silenced culture the opposite is true of the ethnic relations literature which has privileged culture and thereby difference, recreating 'the other' in ways akin to the colonial discourses it seeks to replace. In these accounts culture is understood in a naive and commonsensical way as comprising elements, which allows elements to become variables in the positivist sense. Elements are then ignored or highlighted and people's cultures are re-represented back as marked by specific languages or religious rituals thereby denying the integrity of the whole. These elements are often set against a norm represented by a hegemonic account of national culture. This has given rise to accounts of black people's lives (but not theirs alone) which present their cultures as aberrant or pathological, as exotic and at a great distance from the classes or regions within which they live. Hegemonic cultures are not examined in this way and too often white people assume that they are not part of the discussions of culture or ethnicity. Instead, we need to argue for the view that '. . . culture is a dynamic and multi-textured entity, requiring "thick description", not a set of fixed characteristics which are used to distinguish the normal from the abnormal.'[11]

As Ali Rattansi has argued for Britain, 'Cultural diversity is a central feature of modern British Society'.[12] Recognising this does not necessarily lead towards a more subtle analysis of British society, indeed it may provoke the opposite – a denial and the minister's comments quoted above seem to point in this direction. It is quite clear that 'culture' is not a neutral term and that different values are given to different cultures whether these are based on gender, ethnicity, class or region or religion. It is useful to invoke Bourdieu's work and his emphasis upon cultural capital and cultural competence and the ways in which these are articulated with economic and political power.[13] Adult education is involved in so far as adult education is involved in the reproduction of cultural capitals and cultural competences, but if it is to challenge these powers then counter hegemonic strategies will need to be on the agenda, offering value to a wide range of cultural competencies and demonstrating the means by which cultural capital can be generated. One of the ways in which comparative adult education can assist this process is by not falling into the traps of simple comparisons between cultural groups that has been the hallmark of much of the literature on 'race' and education in Britain so brilliantly critiqued in Rattansi[14] where he shows that in so many studies black is compared to white without taking any account of gender or class let alone patterns of migration and position in the labour market. The model for this type of research is the experimental model where 'all things being equal' two groups are comparable but things are definitely not 'equal' and the complexities are themselves crucial to explanation. It is not possible here to pursue this, but it is possible to call for a more complex and dynamic account of cultures and cultural change which, again drawing on Gramsci's work, is a materialist account.

Conclusion

Those of us who work with black people in Britain are increasingly aware of the limits of our language and our analysis. I use the term black here to describe people of Asian and Afro-Caribbean descent, but it is not intended that this term should deny the specificities of the very diverse cultures and ethnicities that Asian and Afro-Caribbean peoples have nor the diversity of their lives in Britain. However, black people share a common experience of racism in British society despite the fact that they are British (50% of Afro-Caribbean people and 40% of Asian people were born in Britain). Even the term 'Asian' is a colonial term coined by the colonial administration to describe people of Indian descent who were part of the Indian diaspora and who had been transported as indentured labour to places throughout the British empire or encouraged to go as traders to all corners of the world. The term itself ignored the histories, cultures and ethnicities of thousands of people and yet it stands today. It is a term I use here by convention, not by choice.

If our language and our analysis is going to progress then there is clearly an important educational task especially for those involved in comparative work. As Rattansi concludes in relation to schools:

> *Schools may feel powerless to alter a situation in which wider economic and political forces have such a crucial influence. But to ignore these issues would be a serious abnegation of their responsibility in combating racism*

*and giving black communities a fair opportunity to make their rightful
contribution and participate on equal democratic terms as citizens.*[15]

Adult educators have the same responsibilities and those in comparative adult
education more so, but adult education in Britain, at least, has been slow to
intervene at any level. This paper has not been programmatic, but it has
suggested ways in which we can begin to re-think some of our commonsense
assumptions and this activity is itself an intervention.

References
1   B. Anderson, *Imagined Communities: Reflections on the Origin and Spread of Nationalism*, Verso, 1983.
2   S. Hall, 'Minimal selves' in *Identity*, ICA Document 6, Institute of Contemporary Arts, 1987.
3   A. Gramsci, *Selection from the Prison Notebooks of Antonio Gramsci* (ed Q. Hoare and G. Nowell-Smith), Lawrence and Wishart, 1971.
4   *The Guardian*, 14 October 1988.
5   E.W. Said, *Orientalism*, Penguin Books, 1987.
6   R. Inden, 'Orientalist constructions of India', *Modern Asian Studies* 20, 1986.
7   H.K. Bhabha, *The Other Question*, Screen, 1983.
8   R. O'Hanlon, 'Recovering the subject subaltern studies and histories of resistance in colonial south Asia', *Modern Asian Studies* 20, 1986.
9   P. Gilroy, *Their ain't no Black in the Union Jack: the Cultural Politics of Race and Racism*, Hutchinson, 1987.
10 S. Westwood, 'Race, gender and work: black British women in the workplace', *Social Studies Review*, March, 1988.
11 S. Westwood and P. Bhachu (eds), *Enterprising Women: Ethnicity, Economy and Gender Relations*, Routledge, 1988.
12. A. Rattansi, 'Race, education and British society' in R. Dale and associates (eds), *Frameworks for Teaching*, Hodder and Stoughton, 1988.
13 P. Bourdieu, 'Cultural reproduction and social reproduction' in R. Brown (ed), *Knowledge, Education and Cultural Change*, Tavistock, 1974.
14 Rattansi.
15 Rattansi.